Common-sense Morality and Consequentialism

International Library of Philosophy

Editor: Ted Honderich
Professor of Philosophy, University College, London

A catalogue of books already published in the
International Library of Philosophy
will be found at the end of this volume

Common-sense Morality and Consequentialism

by Michael Slote

ROUTLEDGE & KEGAN PAUL

London, Boston, Melbourne and Henley

First published in 1985
by Routledge & Kegan Paul plc
14 Leicester Square, London WC2H 7PH, England
9 Park Street, Boston, Mass. 02108, USA
464 St Kilda Road, Melbourne,
Victoria 3004, Australia and
Broadway House, Newtown Road,
Henley-on-Thames, Oxon RG9 1EN, England

Set in Times, 10 on 12pt
by Input Typesetting Ltd, London
and printed in Great Britain
by St Edmundsbury Press Ltd
Bury St Edmunds, Suffolk

Library of Congress Cataloging in Publication Data

Slote, Michael A.

Common-sense morality and consequentialism.
(International library of philosophy)
Includes index.
1. Ethics. 2. Consequentialism (Ethics) I. Title.
II. Series.
BJ1012.S516 1985   171   84–11438

British Library CIP data also available

ISBN 0–7102–0309–8(c)

For Jenny

CONTENTS

ACKNOWLEDGMENTS

I am indebted to the *Journal of Philosophy* and the *American Philosophical Quarterly* for permission to reprint material in Chapters I and IV, respectively, of the present book; and to the Editor of the Aristotelian Society for permission to make use of material from a symposium (*PAS*, supplementary volume, 1984) in Chapter III. I would also like to thank Olive Murtagh for typing the manuscript and Maria Bagramian for help in proofreading and preparing the index.

INTRODUCTION

Common-sense Morality and Consequentialism seeks to assess the merits of two major forms of moral theory by means of mutual comparison and an attempt to elicit the implications and tendencies of each theory taken individually. Recent attempts to criticize or justify common-sense morality or consequentialism depend on comparisons between these moral views that are taken to show something to the critical advantage or disadvantage of one or the other (or both) of them; and the present book will begin with an attempt to show that these recent discussions inadequately characterize the nature of the dispute between common-sense morality and consequentialism (especially, act-consequentialism) and thereby provide inadequate or incomplete rationales for either of these currently influential kinds of moral theory. The book will go on to examine some tendencies implicit within common-sense morality and consequentialism in order to demonstrate the inherently problematic character of both these moral theories and so give an indication of the immense difficulties that stand in the way of giving a fundamental justification for either of them.

Chapter I begins by considering what has recently been said by philosophers such as Bernard Williams, Thomas Nagel and Samuel Scheffler about the main differences between (utilitarian) act-consequentialism and common-sense morality. Recent discussions focus on common-sense permissions to pursue non-optimific projects and commitments and on common-sense deontological restrictions or 'side-constraints' forbidding killing, maiming, etc., even as a means to preventing many other acts of killing, maiming,

1

etc. (i.e., even in the name of overall optimality); but they ignore another sort of permission that common-sense seems to grant, but ordinary act-consequentialism would deny, namely, permissions to ignore one's own good (or projects) or to prefer someone else's lesser good to one's own greater good. These 'agent-sacrificing permissions' involve a common-sense moral difference between what one may permissibly allow to happen to oneself and what one may permissibly allow to happen to others, and such a self/ other asymmetry is also, I argue, to be found in the deontological restrictions of ordinary morality. What is ordinarily considered morally forbidden to us are acts of killing or harming *others* in the name of overall good consequences: no similar restriction is usually (in secular contexts) thought to exist with respect to the things one may do to *oneself* in the interests of impersonal overall optimality, and this asymmetry is very difficult to account for or justify in ordinary moral terms – e.g., by invoking notions like consent or the common-sense moral need for restricting the individual's natural bias in his own favour or his (selfish) impulses. (Moreover, recent attempts, not to justify, but simply to describe the contours of our common-sense deontological restrictions have ignored the self/other asymmetry and must all, I believe, be qualified accordingly.) Recent work by Nagel, Nozick, and especially Scheffler, has emphasized the difficulty of justifying deontological restrictions quite apart from any consideration of the self/other asymmetry they involve, but the self/other asymmetry of such restrictions (and as it exists outside the area of such restrictions) presents a separate and perhaps equally perplexing problem of justification to defenders of common-sense morality.

Chapter II concentrates on the other sort of divergence between common-sense morality and (act-)consequentialism that has featured in recent discussions: common-sense moral permissions to fulfil one's own non-optimific projects and commitments. Various rationales have been proposed for such permissions, but I argue that they all underestimate the extent of our common-sense moral permissions regarding projects and commitments and the extent to which common-sense morality and act-consequentialism conflict in this area. Our moral permissions here refer not only (e.g.) to projects we are actually interested in or committed to, but to a vast range of possible projects: we are ordinarily supposed to be morally permitted, morally free, to pursue any (innocent) project whatever, a permission that extends to projects we may in fact not be interested in at all. But Bernard Williams's appeal to the integrity of the (moral) agent and other philosophers' emphasis on the unfairness or unreasonableness of the consequentialist demand that one sacrifice one's personal projects in the name of overall optimality, at best justify the agent's permission to pursue the projects he is committed to and offer no explanation of or rationale for the full common-sense permission to pursue any project whatever. Chapter II goes on to suggest that the full range of what common-sense allows here may be justified, instead, by appealing to a plausible notion of (moral) autonomy.

Chapter III considers a possible way of developing (act-)consequentialism that is both of interest in its own right and capable of doing something to mitigate the common-sense moral criticism that act-consequentialism unreasonably restricts the moral autonomy of moral agents (to fulfil whatever innocent projects and commitments they wish). Although act-consequentialism is often defined as a theory that judges the rightness of actions in terms of whether those actions have optimal consequences, consequences as good as those of any alternative action open to the agent, such definitions ignore the distinct possibility of a 'satisficing' form of act-consequentialism that judges the rightness of actions solely in terms of their consequences, but allows a non-optimific action to count as right, if its consequences are good enough (relative, perhaps, to the best consequences the agent could have produced in the circumstances). Optimizing forms of act-consequentialism (and maximizing forms like act-utilitarianism) are not the only possible options for act-consequentialism, and Chapter III seeks to develop and defend the idea of satisficing act-consequentialism by considering some satisficing elements in the common-sense morality of benevolence and by reference to the recent economics literature of individual and firm satisficing. That literature does much to support the idea that individual satisficing (a certain kind of *moderation* on the part of the individual) can sometimes be rational or reasonable. And if certain sorts of deliberate individual non-optimizing and non-maximizing behaviour can be considered rational, then, as I argue in Chapter III, it may be possible to defend the idea of *moral* satisficing, and a satisficing form of act-consequentialism in particular. It will turn out, in fact, that the idea of satisficing consequentialism has a kind of underground previous history in the work of Bentham, Sidgwick, Popper, and others, and one can make better sense of this history once one sees satisficing consequentialism as a distinct conceptual and moral possibility.

In Chapter IV, the distinction between optimizing and satisficing forms of consequentialism is taken as given, and a discussion of the implications of that distinction, which is carried over to Chapter V, is begun. It is argued, in Chapters IV and V, that the distinction between optimizing and satisficing consequentialism very naturally carries us to a point beyond (the need to make) that distinction. Satisficing and optimizing forms of act- or motive-consequentialism involve a choice as to where to draw the line between acts/motives with good enough consequences to count as right/good and acts/motives whose consequences are insufficiently good to count as right/good; and if it can be reasonably argued that any such dividing line is arbitrary, then we may be led to accept a form of act-consequentialism and of motive-consequentialism that does not draw a line between right and wrong or good and not-good and that confines itself (except at the limits) to comparative or scalar judgments of morally better and worse.

What chiefly stands in the way of the move to a (purely) 'scalar' act-consequentialist morality is the idea that (correct) moral principles concerning right and wrong action must be practical and that such a scalar act-morality cannot adequately fulfil the action-guiding function such moral principles are supposed to have. And Chapter IV takes the preliminary, preparatory step of showing that this sort of objection to scalar act-consequentialism is not one that (act-)consequentialists can reasonably make. On the other hand, it has often been thought to be a distinct advantage of common-sense morality (and of moral theory based on common-sense morality) that it requires principles concerning right and wrong action (as opposed to those covering motives or states of character) to be action-guiding, and Chapter IV argues, to the contrary, that some of the most central principles of right and wrong action that ordinary morality subscribes to cannot plausibly be expected to guide action.

Once the non-practical character of various consequentialist and non-consequentialist principles of right and wrong action is established, in Chapter IV, we are ready to go on, in Chapter V to argue in favour not only of scalar forms of act-consequentialism

4

and motive-consequentialism, but also of a scalar form of our common-sense morality of benevolence. The question just how much of our time or money we ought, morally, to give to those less fortunate than ourselves may not admit of the sort of definite answer that has so often been sought (or given) in this area, and we may be limited, in terms of the objective claims of common-sense morality, to judgments of morally better and worse, with regard to benevolent giving. However, although Chapter V pushes ahead in the aforementioned directions, I should point out here, as I explain at greater length later in the book, that the scepticism of Chapter V seems somewhat suspect – by comparison, say, with the idea of moral satisficing in Chapter III. I think we have reason to resist the claim (e.g.) that consequentialism as an (attempt at) objective moral theory should limit itself to comparative judgments, and the argument of Chapters IV and V is intended as much to elicit a reply from within consequentialism as to prove that consequentialism must proceed in a certain attenuating direction. But I have no idea myself what sort of form such a reply should or could take, and although I prefer to think that consequentialism is best developed in non-scalar form and also hope and believe that satisficing consequentialism holds out promising possibilities for consequentialism, we likewise need to face the problems raised by the idea of scalar consequentialism and by those plausible, natural assumptions, employed in Chapters IV and V, that seem to lead in *that* direction.

But the problems of consequentialism are by no means limited to those raised in Chapters IV and V. The fact that consequentialist moral evaluation can be applied, separately, to both motives and actions and that a consequentialist is likely to be a motive-consequentialist and an act-consequentialist at the same time raises some familiar, important problems about the possibilities of conflict between these two 'levels' of consequentialist evaluation. A loving parent who is also an act-consequentialist may face a problem in deciding whether to do the consequentialistically right act of saving three drowning strangers or to act upon his desire to save his own child, who is also drowning. If love dictates saving his own child and is, in motive-consequentialist terms, the best motive for him to have in general, he must choose between an act that seems justified in terms of motive-consequentialism and one that seems justified in terms of act-consequentialism; and in recent years various philosophers have considered the question which of these putative forms of justification takes precedence (or is acceptable) for the consistent consequentialist.

Chapter VI of the present book argues that, perhaps contrary to initial expectations, consequentialism cannot consistently treat wrong acts as justified in consequentialist terms, even when such acts are motivated by a consequentialistically good or best motive. This 'solution' to the above conflict is shown to resemble closely what has recently, increasingly, been taken to be the correct diagnosis of where rule-utilitarianism goes astray. But the solution is then itself called into question by a new possibility for consequentialist moral theory, the possibility, namely, that consequentialism's seeming preference for an impersonal and even atemporal standpoint of moral evaluation is best realized, not by theories like act-consequentialism and motive-consequentialism, which, even when accepted together, make separate evaluations of acts and motives, but rather by consequentialist theories that evaluate total historical patterns of action-cum-motivation. And such theories, it is then argued, naturally lead one still further along the road of impersonality and objectivity to a point where consequentialism as a theory evaluating agent-factors in terms of their consequences vanishes and one is left simply with (what Amartya Sen calls) an 'outcome morality' that comparatively evaluates different total universal histories but cannot meaningfully be treated as a morality (moral theory) at all. Again, such a conclusion is one that the consequentialist, perhaps all of us, have reason to resist; but the argument of Chapter VI is intended to show how difficult it is to prevent consequentialism from swallowing its own tail in the above way, once one treats the *sub specie aeternitatis* standpoint as the fulcrum for all moral judgments and justification and once one holds, as consequentialists also tend to do, that the valid (utilitarian) consequentialist standard of morality need not function as a practical guide for moral agents.

After the lengthy treatment of consequentialist moral theory, Chapter VII returns the discussion to the area of common-sense morality and focuses on some further difficulties in that area. Common-sense morality faces problems in relation to deontological restrictions and a self/other asymmetry that can both be criticized (as we see in Chapter I) for putting insufficient weight on good consequences; but Chapter VII discusses the precisely oppo-

[handwritten margin notes: the Archimedean point. ie as 5th knowledge which is motivating.]

6

site objection that by allowing for certain kinds of 'moral luck' common-sense morality allows consequences too much weight in the evaluation of agents and actions. Ordinary people treat people and actions as morally worse or better, as more or less culpable, depending on whether, e.g., some act of negligence or attempt to murder actually has or lacks certain bad consequences; and yet it also seems plausible, in common-sense terms, to hold that actual consequences, mere luck or accident, cannot affect the moral character of acts or agents. It is very difficult to know how to settle this internal conflict of common-sense moral thinking; but it is argued, in Chapter VII, that the question whether we should accept this sort of moral luck is best considered in the light of a more general issue concerning the possibility of what I call 'covert (temporal) relationality'. Whether, for example, a republic was founded and existed in America on 4 July 1776 seems to depend on events subsequent to that date, in particular, on the ultimate success of the American Revolution, yet without focusing on such examples, it seems natural to hold that whether there is a republic in a certain place at a certain time is a matter only of what is intrinsic to that time and place and cannot depend on any relation to what comes later. Granting the existence of such dependence, we have an example of what may be called covert relationality, and Chapter VII offers a number of putative examples of such relationality and attempts to establish that moral luck – and the further possibility that the morality of someone's actions at one time may depend on what that person does (deliberately, and not through luck) subsequently – are best viewed as instances of covert relationality. This serves to make moral luck seem slightly less idiosyncratic and unacceptable, but raises important further questions about covert relationality that cannot be answered within the present work.

The book's conclusion attempts, first, to draw a number of parallels – some already mentioned, some new – between points made in earlier chapters about morality and points that can be made about individual (extramoral) rationality; and then goes on to compare the aims, methods, and results of *Common-sense Morality and Consequentialism* with those of Sidgwick's great book. In what follows here, I am perhaps more critical of (utilitarian) consequentialism than Sidgwick was, or wished to be; but this critical attitude is not directed in favour of any alternative theory like common-sense morality, and, in the end, all the criticism is intended to encourage, rather than preclude, the further, more adequate development of both common-sense morality and consequentialism as moral theories.

I

COMMON-SENSE MORALITY
AND CONSEQUENTIALISM

1

One of the most notable features of act-utilitarianism and of act-consequentialism generally[1] is its appeal from the standpoint of impersonal benevolence. When (and if) we abstract from our *must it be benevolence?* particular identities and our personal desires and concerns, and view what happens in the world benevolently but as it were from outside, we wish for optimific acts to be performed and are glad when they are performed. And such acts are the acts which act-utilitarianism and act-consequentialism designate as morally right or obligatory.[2]

On the other hand, common-sense morality differs from utilitarianism and from consequentialism generally in holding that certain kinds of acts are morally obligatory even when they produce less overall good than certain alternatives open to a given agent, and the prime illustration of such obligations has been those moral 'side constraints' which dictate, for example, that one may not kill an innocent person even if doing so will save five innocent lives, indeed even if it will prevent the killing of five *other* innocent people by people other than oneself. Here it is assumed that acceptance of the side-constraints involves accepting the idea that killing can be a wrong thing to *do* even when from an impersonal standpoint a better state of affairs (series of events) will *occur* if one does kill, and clearly such deontological restrictions on what a person may do even in the name of maximizing the good are involved in the morality most people accept.

9

But recent discussions have also focused on another common-sense exception to the utilitarian (consequentialist) notion that considerations of what is best from an impersonal standpoint decide what actions are obligatory. For common-sense also presumably permits each agent to give some preference to his own concerns, projects and commitments even when that prevents him from producing the objectively best state(s) of affairs he is capable of bringing about and thus from acting as impersonal benevolence would prefer.

In recent discussions philosophers such as Bernard Williams, Thomas Nagel, and Samuel Scheffler have tended to assume that these two non-consequentialist elements in ordinary morality are the two main ways in which such morality diverges from consequentialism and have attempted to see to what extent these divergences from the impersonal standpoint can be justified.[3] However, these recent discussions ignore an important further anti-consequentialist element in common-sense morality that we must take into account in order to understand (and perhaps justify) the various ways ordinary morality differs from what a utilitarian or impersonal outlook dictates.

This further, and ultimately, I believe, highly perplexing element of common-sense morality consists in the permissibility, according to ordinary moral thinking, of *not* benefiting *oneself* and of favouring *other people* even when this leads to less than optimal results. If I have a choice between conferring a great benefit on myself or a lesser benefit on someone else, and these are the only relevant factors in the situation, common-sense morality tells us that it is perfectly permissible to sacrifice one's own greater benefit to the lesser benefit of another. In the absence of some special relation or obligation to that other, common-sense might concede it was irrational, stupid or gratuitous to do so, but surely not that it was morally wrong. Similarly, in a situation where no one else is concerned (or even, if you will, where no one else exists) if I ignore an opportunity to enjoy a pleasure or do not bother to avoid a pain, then (other things equal) I do wrong by consequentialist standards, but, again, not by ordinary standards. Thus ordinary moral thinking seems to involve an asymmetry regarding what an agent is permitted to do to himself and what he is permitted to do to others. If one could easily prevent someone else's pain, it is typically thought wrong not to

10

do so, but not to avoid a similar pain in oneself is only lazy, crazy, or senseless, not wrong. And by the same token, there are cases where it is thought obligatory (wrong not) to prevent the greater pain of another rather than the much lesser pain of oneself, but again, it is only irrational or stupid or terribly selfless to allow a greater pain to oneself knowing that someone else will avoid a lesser one as a result.

This asymmetry represents an anti-consequentialist element in ordinary morality that is almost entirely ignored in recent discussions of the relation between such morality and consequentialism. Those discussions have considered the nature and justification of supposed deontological restrictions (side-constraints) on human action which in certain circumstances forbid the maximization of impersonally-considered good. And they have considered the nature and justification of supposed permissions to favour one's own projects and concerns rather than always seek the impersonally-judged overall best state of things (call these *agent-favouring* permissions). But they have not focused on another sort of permission that common-sense equally allows to individuals, (self-other-asymmetric) permissions sometimes to sacrifice or remain indifferent to *one's own* pain or harm or failures even when this leads to less good results overall (call these *agent-sacrificing* permissions).

It is worth noting how deep these just-mentioned permissions go in our common moral thinking. For example, common-sense morality recommends and in many cases requires benevolence (beneficence) from agents, but acting benevolently is not the same thing as maximizing the good. A person who does something for himself, when he is in no position to do anything for anyone else or anything better for himself, is not acting benevolently (to himself), whereas one who favours others over himself *is* benevolent; and that is because the term 'benevolent' only applies to what we do for or give to *others*. The fact that we have a word like 'benevolence' that behaves this way shows, I think, how deeply the asymmetry between what one may do to others and to oneself is felt in our common morality; it reflects the deep sense that there is nothing morally wrong with favouring others or being indifferent to one's own well-being (except insofar as doing so goes against other duties, e.g., a promise to take care of oneself, or makes one less able to help others). (Utilitarianism, which makes it a moral obligation to help oneself where no one else can be affected for better or worse, does not, strictly speaking, recommend benevolence, but rather a kind of 'impersonal benevolence' which, by imaginatively placing the agent outside the universe, makes the benefits he seeks to distribute to himself and others in the universe seem a kind of giving to and doing for others.)

Agent-sacrificing anti-consequentialist permissions have not always, however, been ignored by philosophers. W. D. Ross, for example, discusses these permissions at some length, accepting their validity and even attempting to explain why utilitarianism fails to take them into account.[4] Ross did not feel the need to justify the various non-consequentialist elements he found in common-sense morality except by reference to intuition, but recent criticism of utilitarianism and consequentialism – perhaps granting the consequentialist standpoint an intuitive force and prima facie plausibility that Ross would have been unwilling to allow – has sought to give a reasoned account of or justification for the non-consequentialism of ordinary morality and to show, in particular, that agent-morality need not be regulated or conceived from an impersonal standpoint. The obstacles to completing such an account or justification have also been discussed, but my point here is that in the light of the agent-sacrificing permissions, this task of motivating and justifying common-sense morality becomes even more complicated and difficult than has been imagined.

Agent-sacrificing permissions are clearly unacceptable from the standpoint of impersonal morality, for strict consequentialism must hold that one is not (other things being equal) permitted to sacrifice one's own (greater) good (for the sake of another's lesser good). By the same token, any consequentialist moral conception that embodies an impersonal standpoint will surely refuse to countenance an asymmetry, between what an agent may do to himself and what he may do to others, that makes no difference to the overall goodness of what happens. I believe, moreover, that unease about agent-sacrificing permissions is especially likely to focus on the asymmetry they involve, once we recognize the important role that that asymmetry plays in the deontological side-constraints of ordinary morality. Although the point is frequently ignored or (as we shall see) implicitly denied in discussions of side-constraints on what an agent may permissibly do in the name of optimality, many of the sorts of things common-sense morality forbids us to do to others it *does not* forbid us to do to ourselves. Even if one may not cut up another person to furnish healthy organs that will save the lives of five injured or sick individuals, there is no immediate moral bar to cutting oneself up in order to save five other people.[5] There is no fundamental moral reason why someone should not sacrifice *himself* to save five people who need organ transplants, and the side-constraints built into ordinary morality concern only harm *done to others* in the name of good results.

Now although some problematic aspects of deontological restrictions have been pointed out in the past,[6] no one has remarked on the odd asymmetry they involve between what an agent is permitted to do to others and what he may do to himself. It has been said that if the killing of an innocent person is so objectionable, it is odd that it should be objectionable for someone to act in such a way as to minimize such objectionable acts [by killing one (other) person in order to prevent five other killings]. But there is additional oddness – especially, but, as we shall see, not merely, from an impersonal consequentialist standpoint – in supposing further that although one may not kill another person to prevent five killings, one *may* kill a person in such a cause if that person is oneself.[7] Common-sense deontology is thus more complexly and problematically contoured than it has been said to be.

Moreover, like the asymmetry regarding harms and benefits mentioned above, the deontological self-other asymmetry – far from being a superficial element of ordinary morality – is reflected in the very language of moral criticism. Just as the term 'benevolence' rests on an asymmetry between doing for others and doing for oneself, so too, for example, do words like 'murder' and 'injustice' make a (deontological) distinction between what one does to others and what one does to oneself. Suicide, for example, is not murder, and as has been noted at least since Aristotle, it is difficult, if not impossible, to imagine a situation in which someone treats himself unjustly[8] (or, for that matter, in which someone *violates* his own rights). These linguistic distinctions presumably reflect deep-seated assumptions of common-sense morality, but it is of course open to us to stop using such language and/or to reject its underlying moral presuppositions.[9] If, however, we reject the self-other asymmetry, we must recognize what we are doing and see, in particular, that that asymmetry has a double place within ordinary morality. It is not only, as we saw earlier, an asymmetry in the morality of allocating harms and benefits that treats it as somehow morally better to disregard a potential harm or benefit to oneself than to disregard one to someone else; but also represents a qualification in deontological restrictions against *doing* certain things to people that treats what one does to others as morally different from what one does to oneself.[10] As we have seen, neither of these aspects of the self-other asymmetry can be made sense of in act-consequentialist terms; from the impersonal standpoint there is no reason for it to make an (immediate) difference whether a given act concerns the agent or another person.[11]

But the oddness of the asymmetry is not entirely due to consequentialist considerations and the adoption of the impersonal standpoint. Ordinary morality (unlike act-utilitarianism) treats our obligations to others as dependent on how near they stand to us in relations of affection or special commitment; the strength of our obligations to our immediate family is (other things being equal) greater than to relations generally, our obligations to friends and relations greater than to compatriots generally, and our obligations to the latter, in turn, greater than to the people of other countries.

Ordinary morality thereby immediately reflects the normal structure of an adult individual's concerns. We are naturally more concerned about and have more reason to be concerned about the well-being of friends and relations than of more distant others, and common-sense morality seems to build such differences into the varyingly strong duties it assigns us to concern ourselves with the well-being of others.[12] However, by means of the self-other asymmetry common-sense morality also superimposes an absolute moral discontinuity on the structure of concern in which each agent is normally situated. On the other hand, it encourages the idea that strength of obligation weakens as one gets further from the agent, but on the other hand, and in seeming opposition to the first idea, it assumes that there is no moral obligation whatever (except indirectly) for the agent to benefit *himself* or concern himself with his *own* projects. Once one leaves the agent himself behind the agent's obligations vary in proportion to his reason for concern, but where he has greatest reason for concern in the natural course of things, he has no direct obligation whatever. I

14

submit that this appears odd and unmotivated even apart from consequentialist considerations (although consequentialism provides a way of avoiding the oddness); yet the above discontinuity within the natural structure of our concern seems integral to common-sense moral thinking. Having, however, pointed out the oddness of the self-other asymmetry both from the impersonal standpoint and for other reasons, let me now indicate some of the problems that beset those who ignore the asymmetry in their discussions of deontological restrictions on actions.

2

However problematic the self-other asymmetry may be, it is part of common-sense morality. Yet those concerned with the ways in which common-sense morality diverges from impersonal conse-quentialism have failed to focus on the asymmetry and in particular on the permissions it allows an agent to do to himself things it would be considered wrong for him to do to others. This fact has repercussions for recent attempts to understand common-sense morality. There have, for example, been many efforts over the years to state acceptable deontological constraints on behaviour that are in tune with our intuitions over a wide spectrum of cases. These attempts do not so much seek to justify the constraints as to state the criteria of permissible harming and allowing of harm that are endemic to our ordinary thought about these things and that are elicited by seeking a variety of moral examples to test intuitions against. Thus in recent years the attempt to square particular cases with common-sense intuitions has led many people to treat the side-constraints on killing the innocent as less than absolute; to prevent an absolute and world-shaking catastrophe, common-sense may allow the killing of the innocent,[13] and in a similar vein, Judith Thomson has recently argued that even where no such catastrophe threatens, it is some-times permissible to kill (bring about the death of) innocent people: one may, she thinks, deflect a runaway train so that one person is killed rather than the five people on the track the train is already on.[14] Still others have invoked the 'doctrine of double effect' and argued (roughly) that one may kill innocent people when that is a foreseen but unintended consequence of some

15

sufficiently good end (tactical bombing in wartime), but not when it is a means to a good end (terror bombing).

Now as more and more cases of killing and letting die are considered, the attempt to give a precise statement of common-sense deontological restrictions on killing yields more and more complex qualifications. It seems to turn out, for example, that it is not killing one innocent person as a means of preventing five other such killings that is forbidden, but rather something far more qualified that is forbidden (even as the means to prevent many more actions of the same highly qualified kind). Some have argued that the distinctions involved in these qualifications are insupportably vague or senseless; others that these distinctions do not carry the moral weight that side-constraints are supposed to carry.[15] But in any case the consideration of cases and winnowing of covering principles continues even to the present and in great part it is fuelled by a conviction, which it is no part of my purpose to undermine here, that we ought to find out what our intuitions about particular cases are as an (one) initial step towards a theoretical understanding of right and wrong.

But once one takes notice of the self-other asymmetry, it becomes clear that various attempts to formulate what is enshrined in ordinary deontological thinking contain (at least) one qualification too few. When, for example, Judith Thomson distinguishes cases where one deflects a runaway trolley so that it kills fewer people from cases where one kills and injures a person as a means to stopping such a trolley, by saying that one may do something to a force (deflect it) in order to prevent many deaths, even if that involves one in killing some smaller number of people, but may not do something to a person to stop a force, she ignores the difference it makes whether it is oneself or another person to whom one does something in order to stop a force. A person may permissibly sacrifice *himself* in order to stop a life-threatening force, and so accounts of deontological restrictions, like Thomson's, that ignore the self-other distinction fail to articulate the precise contours of those restrictions.

Faithfulness to our intuitions, then, requires that Thomson modify what she says and claim only that one may do to a force what one may not do to *another* person, but the qualification itself raises questions, calls for explanation. And the need for an explanation, and the problematic character of what needs explai-

16

ning, become all the more obvious when we see how many other attempts to articulate the deontological restrictions of common morality need similar qualification. Quite recently, for example, James Montmarquet, in reply to Thomson, has claimed that the real criterion for permission to kill is that one may do so to those already at risk in order to prevent a greater number of deaths, but not to those who are not already at risk.[16] But again it is necessary to make a qualification to allow a person not at risk to sacrifice *himself* as a means to minimizing the loss of life. Similarly, when an attempt is made to articulate the deontological restrictions on action which are commonly associated with the doctrine of double effect, and it is said (e.g.) that one may bring about a good thing that one foresees will have harmful consequences, but may not do harm as a means to that same good, a qualification is needed to accommodate our sense that people may permissibly harm themselves as a means to a greater objective good.

It would be irrelevant at this point to protest that those who offered these formulations had this sort of qualification implicitly in mind. Perhaps they did, but by not stating the qualification, the issues about what underlies our deontological side-constraints were not only obscured but misperceived. Thus Thomson's view of deontological restrictions at the very least implies that it is the difference between person and force that underlies and explains such restrictions, but this view cannot possibly survive consideration of what someone may permissibly do to himself. The self-other distinction is an important factor in determining what we may or may not do to a person, and so although what one may do in runaway trolley cases may partly depend on the force-person distinction, it also depends on the self-other distinction. Making the necessary qualification explicit helps to make it clear that any explanation of our intuitions about such cases must be more complex than Thomson suggests; for it must among other things take account of the self-other distinction and explain why that should make a difference.

The failure to see clearly enough that the self-other distinction is involved in the deontological restrictions on what an agent does vitiates other recent attempts to articulate and motivate those restrictions. Thus Nagel in his Tanner Lectures speaks of the deontological restrictions as concerning what one may do to *others*; but he does not call attention to the asymmetry between self and other that this implies, and when he attempts to explain the principle of double effect and deontological restrictions generally, the explanation offered effectively rules out such an asymmetry. Nagel holds that the force of the doctrine of double effect derives from the internal viewpoint of an agent, as opposed to the external impersonal standpoint that considers only what is happening (as a result of what one does) rather than what one is intentionally doing (or allowing). According to Nagel, when we adopt the agential standpoint, an appropriately formulated doctrine of double effect appeals to us because to go against it is to be guided by evil. Someone who intentionally does (or, according to Nagel, allows) evil for the sake of good is allowing himself to be guided by evil, is making what he does a positive rather than a negative function of evil. When he aims at good via this evil, he is swimming against the normative current and it is no wonder, Nagel thinks, that this should produce in an agent the sense of doing something awful. This sort of explanation produces the right results for the case Nagel mentions where the only way to get badly injured friends to the hospital involves producing pain in a child. But Nagel holds that pain is an objective evil, and presumably if I produce pain in myself in order to help someone else avoid an even greater evil, the pain I suffer is a personal evil and represents a personal sacrifice even if I do choose to undergo it. Nagel's explanation of the deontological restrictions implies, however, that one may not permissibly hurt or give pain to oneself in order to save someone from a greater evil, since in this case too one is swimming against the current of value. And this conclusion runs counter to the ordinary intuitions Nagel says he is trying to account for. Such self-affecting examples clearly vitiate the sort of explanation Nagel gives, and, once again, the failure results from insufficient attention to the moral asymmetry between what one may do to oneself and what one may do to others.

Attempts to explain our deontological side-constraints (Nagel's among them) have been previously criticized for their tendency to rely on some special dignity or value of human beings (or human lives) – the objection being that if humans are so special, that may actually give us a reason (e.g.) to minimize the death of such valuable entities and thus to kill one person in order to prevent the killing of five other people.[17] But the present criticism of Nagel's and other attempts to explain and motivate our actual deontological side-constraints focuses on a previously unnoticed but related aspect of their failure: the specialness of persons or (as in Nagel's case) the irreducible validity of the personal standpoint simply cannot explain why, acting from a personal standpoint, an agent may not do to special and valuable others what he may do to the equally special and valuable person who is himself.

It is often said that common-sense gives morally different weight to commissions and omissions, treating doing harm as worse than not preventing harm (or not helping), killing as worse than letting die, etc.; and another way of putting what I have been saying would be to point out that any articulation of what is implicit in these just-mentioned distinctions must contain a qualification indicating the difference between self and other. It may in general be wrong to harm another person in order to prevent harm to different people, but there seems to be nothing wrong with harming oneself in order to prevent harm to third parties; and once one recognizes that the articulation of our ordinary morality constantly requires the qualification '*other* people' in stating what may not be done, I think it is difficult to avoid the feeling that this constant refrain needs some sort of explanation. The deontological restrictions of ordinary morality thus contain an asymmetry that must itself be explained if any satisfactory explanation of the restrictions themselves and of our actual morality as a whole is to be forthcoming. And in the light of the self-other asymmetry, common-sense morality appears more complex, more difficult to justify, and as a whole more problematic than those who have defended common-sense morality against consequentialism have recognized. Ordinary moral thinking makes room for agent-favouring permissions to pursue one's own life plans and interests, for duties (and supererogations) of benevolence (beneficence) involving a self-other asymmetry, and for deontological restrictions also involving such an asymmetry; and any attempt to motivate ordinary morality (as it diverges from consequentialism or utilitarianism) must take account of all these elements.

Previous attempts to justify ordinary morality have focused on difficulties in justifying deontological side-constraints that appear to be independent of the self-other asymmetry, but as a general phenomenon, the asymmetry itself is difficult to motivate or explain, more difficult, in fact, than might initially appear. It seems incapable, for example, of being motivated by the sorts of considerations that have recently been put forward in defence of agent-favouring permissions. Williams's appeal to the integrity of agents[18] and Scheffler's to the natural independence of the personal point of view[19] may argue in favour of (sometimes) allowing agents to follow their own personal projects and concerns at the expense of impersonally judged overall optimality, but they hardly seem capable of justifying permissions to *sacrifice one's own* projects, interests, or concerns. Of course, if someone is a masochist with a higher-order project of frustrating some of his lower-order concerns, then arguments from integrity, etc., might conceivably justify a permission to do so, but even where an agent is not a masochist and (seemingly gratuitous) self-sacrifice is not called for by her personal projects or concerns, common-sense morality treats such sacrifice as permissible. In certain circumstances where an agent would in fact be unwilling (given her life concerns) to permit herself to be harmed, common-sense morality permits her to allow herself to be harmed, but, asymmetrically, forbids her to allow such harm to others; and this permission and this asymmetry cannot presumably be derived from attempts to justify people in taking special interest in or giving special weight to their own projects and commitments.

On the other hand, it has been suggested to me that the reason why we are allowed to harm ourselves or avoid some benefit, where we would not be permitted to harm another person or prevent her from receiving a similar benefit, lies in the consent implicit in actions we do to ourselves. If I harm myself or avoid a benefit, I presumably do this willingly, whereas the agent whom I refuse to benefit does not consent to this neglect (and when she does there is nothing wrong with what I do). It might then be thought that the moral asymmetry we have noted is not a deep feature of morality but rather derivative from and justifiable in terms of the moral importance of consent.

But such an explanation is not really sufficient to explain our common-sense moral asymmetry. If someone irrationally asks me to harm or kill him, it will presumably be irrational and wrong of me to kill him, more wrong at any rate than if I irrationally choose to kill myself; yet the consent seems equal in the two cases.[20] Similarly, it makes a significant difference, in common-sense moral terms, whether I negligently cause another person unwanted harm or negligently do so to myself. Yet consent seems *equally absent* in these two cases. Finally, and perhaps most persuasively, if I can either avoid an enduring pain to myself or a short-lived one to you, you and I might both agree that it would be foolish of me to prevent the shorter one to you; judging the matter objectively, you might not consent to my taking the longer pain upon myself in order to save you from the shorter pain. Yet there would be nothing morally wrong, from a common-sense standpoint, in such a sacrifice. But when positions are reversed and I can avoid a short-lived pain to myself or a longer one to you and it is morally right that I should do the latter, you will presumably not consent to my doing the former and it will be wrong if I do so. Again, consent or lack of consent seems not to make the relevant common-sense moral difference. The self-other moral asymmetry eludes the distinction between consent and non-consent, and is thus not easy to account for.

Explanations of the origins of ordinary morality that stress its necessity to general well-being seem likewise incapable of accounting for (much less justifying) the self-other asymmetry of such morality. Thus G. J. Warnock has said that the 'object of morality' is to better the human predicament by seeking to countervail our limited sympathies (our tendency to prefer ourselves or some small group including ourselves).[21] The self-other asymmetry indeed suggests that common morality seeks to counter our limited sympathies, but it also indicates that the countering of such sympathies is not precisely equivalent to the general goal of bettering the human predicament. Improvement of the agent's situation can be part of the betterment of the human predicament, but is not in any obvious way part of the attempt to countervail the agent's limited sympathies. Perhaps, then, in order to justify or explain the permission to ignore one's own well-being and the self-other asymmetry generally, we must treat the countervailing of limited sympathies as the fundamental 'object of morality' rather than (*pace* Warnock) as a means towards the general amelioration of the human predicament. But such a justification/explanation needs a lot of work: after all, why should morality be concerned with countervailing limited human sympathies *except* as a means to general well-being (the betterment of the human predicament generally)?[22]

Of course, even apart from the difficulty of motivating the self-other asymmetry, the justification of common-sense morality faces many other problems. Various problematic features of deontological restrictions have been brought to light in recent years, and the obstacles to motivating such restrictions – quite independently of the self-other asymmetry they involve – have lately been much emphasized. Indeed, attempts to motivate agent-favouring permissions seem on the whole to have been far more successful than attempts to motivate commonsense deontological restrictions, and I can at present think of no promising way to provide a rationale either for deontological restrictions or for the self-other asymmetry that is involved in such restrictions but clearly has wider moral application. I suspect that the defender of common-sense morality may at this point want to claim that such rationales are unnecessary because common-sense morality has an intuitive plausibility which, even if insufficient to destroy the appeal of the impersonal standpoint, can stand up to it without withering in its icy objective glare; but on the other hand he might well feel that consequentialism is so forceful and so well motivated that the anti-consequentialist elements of common-sense morality do stand in need of a philosophical justification. And once it is seen that the task of justification, in addition to its other, more familiar obstacles, involves the new problem of motivating the self-other asymmetry, he will not, I think, be tempted to underestimate its difficulty.

II

MORAL AUTONOMY

1

As I mentioned in the last chapter, various recently offered rationales for common-sense permissions to pursue non-optimific life
projects or commitments have seemed (or been held) to meet
with greater success than attempts to justify common-sense deontological restrictions. The rationales for the common-sense permissions have involved an attempt to explain where act-utilitarianism
and act-consequentialism generally go wrong in denying such
permissions. But I hope in the present chapter to show that these
critiques of consequentialism have been wrongly focused. They
have underestimated the *extent* to which act-consequentialism
infringes the permissions ordinary, or common-sense, morality
grants to moral agents, and they have, partly in consequence,
offered inadequate rationales (even from a common-sense standpoint) for the moral freedom to pursue non-optimific projects and
commitments. The fundamental explanation and justification of
such permissions, indeed of all common-sense contra-utilitarian
permissions, turns out to involve the familiar notion of autonomy.[1]

However, in order to justify an approach in terms of autonomy
and distinguish it from previous attempts to provide justification
for the pursuit of non-optimific personal projects, plans, and
commitments, we shall have to focus on an area of divergence
between common-sense morality and act-consequentialism that
has been ignored in recent discussions. Attempts recently to
defend or deny common-sense permissions to pursue projects and

23

commitments non-optimifically have taken no notice of another class of permissions that common-sense grants but act-utilitarianism denies, namely, the agent-sacrificing permissions mentioned in Chapter I. And once this new class of permissions is taken into account, we shall be better able to understand the locus of disagreement between utilitarianism and common-sense morality and the actual rationale of common-sense permissions to pursue non-optimific projects and commitments.

Now, as I also mentioned in Chapter I, this new class of common-sense permissions cannot entirely be subsumed under those common-sense permissions to pursue personal projects and permissions that have been so much stressed in recent criticism of utilitarianism and consequentialism. If a given person's project is precisely to benefit others even, if necessary, at his own expense (i.e., at some cost to him of ease, or pleasure, or material well-being) or if he has the higher-order masochistic aim/project of foiling some of his first-order aims or desires, then his moral permission to favour others or ignore his own well-being may be a special case (however deviant) of the common-sense permission to pursue one's own projects and commitments. But not all permissions non-optimifically to favour others over oneself or to avoid personal benefits can be justified in this way.

Some people have no intention of or interest in avoiding benefits or promoting other people's lesser, in preference to their own greater, good; indeed their life plans may be incompatible with such behaviour. Yet if we are to speak at all of permissions agents have to do things that they have no desire to do (e.g., to pursue the general welfare when they have no intention of doing so) – as surely we must do in moral theory, then it must be acknowledged that the above-mentioned common-sense permissions to favour others or ignore one's own well-being extend not only to those inclined to act on such permissions but also to those who have no intention of doing so. So the permission which (according to common-sense morality) an agent bent on his own (selfish) projects and commitments has either simply to sacrifice his own well-being or to sacrifice his own greater well-being in the name of other people's lesser well-being cannot derive from any moral permission he has to pursue the projects he holds most dear.[2] If such permissions exist, they are not subsumable under the permission to pursue one's own deepest interests, for they exist as permissions to do certain things that are not among – and are even incompatible with – the agent's projects or interests. That is why it is appropriate to call them *agent-sacrificing permissions*.

Now, as far as I can tell, this class of permissions can neither be explained nor justified in terms of the usual sorts of rationales that have been offered in favour of common-sense permissions to pursue one's own non-optimific projects and commitments. Bernard Williams has argued, for example, that the act-utilitarian moral proscription of the pursuit of non-optimal projects and commitments alienates a moral agent from his own deepest identity and is an attack on what as an individual he most deeply is, on his integrity.[3] Others have suggested that to deny an individual the moral permission or right to pursue his own (non-optimific) projects and concerns is to demand too much of a sacrifice from moral agents, is to make unfair or unreasonable demands on moral individuals.[4] But considerations of these sorts cannot justify or explain the new class of permission I have been speaking of in the face of a utilitarianism that denies them. Act-utilitarianism and act-consequentialism require, for example, that an agent (with no desire to avoid benefits or favour others over himself) should not favour others over himself when he can accomplish more overall good by helping himself alone; it denies such an agent permission to make such a sacrifice, yet in so doing, it hardly lays an unfair burden on that agent or in any way interferes with his deepest commitments or his integrity, for *ex hypothesi* he has no interest in making the sacrifice that common-sense allows him. So at this point, unless we wish to consider denying the validity of such agent-sacrificing permissions, we need to account for them independently of the usual justifications for permissions to pursue projects and commitments. Of course, there may at first seem to be something odd about permissions to do things one has no actual interest in doing, things inconsistent with one's actual life plans or commitments, and in consequence the option of dismissing such permissions as illusory may initially appear attractive. But it will become clear in what follows that agent-sacrificing permissions are not, in fact, particularly odd or atypical, and so cannot so easily be dismissed or ignored. I think we should look again at permissions to pursue life projects and commitments, this time in the light of the agent-sacrificing permissions mentioned above. And once we do, I think we shall see that even permissions to pursue personal projects and commitments cannot properly be explained or justified in terms of integrity or the unreasonable demandingness of act-utilitarianism. Rather, it will turn out that they are to be understood in basically the same way as agent-sacrificing permissions. All common-sense permissions (except those based on deontological restrictions or obligations) will be then accounted for in a unified way.

2

What now needs showing is that even the permissibility of pursuing a life project or commitment of one's own is not, most fundamentally, to be justified in terms either of integrity or of what morality can reasonably demand of an agent in the way of self-sacrifice. Our permission to pursue non-optimal projects, concerns and commitments has been too narrowly conceived and once one recognizes the full extent of such permissions (as ordinary morality conceives them), one is forced to justify them in other terms.

The clue to this excessive narrowness comes, in fact, from what we have just said about 'agent-sacrificing' permissions. For these involve a moral freedom to act *against* an agent's own projects and commitments that the agent himself is not willing to act upon. But some of the common-sense permissions that we have to pursue certain projects and commitments (I shall in what follows simplify by concentrating exclusively on projects) are also of this sort. Take a person committed to research in epistemology, whose career project is to pursue research in this field and perhaps to write a book along certain roughly-given lines. If justifications in terms of integrity or unreasonable sacrifice are valid, then he has permission to pursue these projects of his even if from a universal impersonal point of view it is not for the best that he do so. But from the standpoint of common-sense morality these are not the only permissions this agent has, in the circumstances. Just as common sense grants that a person not actually interested in favouring others may be morally permitted to do so, surely common-sense morality also allows that a person actually interested in one sort of project may be morally permitted to pursue *some other project*. For example, with regard to the person interested in going further in epistemology, common sense surely grants that it would not be wrong for him to pursue some other project than the one he is in fact interested in, a project, say, in the history of philosophy. Before I have chosen some particular career, common-sense tells us, I have the moral freedom to choose and devote myself to any (innocent) career or life project I wish.[5] I am permitted to devote myself to epistemology, am permitted to devote myself to the history of philosophy, am permitted to devote myself to painting, etc. But these indefinitely many permissions do not – all but one – vanish when I choose and commit myself to one of these possible projects or careers. Even if at some point a person becomes interested in and committed to pursuing a career in epistemology, common-sense would tell us that it is still permissible for the person to pursue some other project, that it would not be wrong for him, e.g., to abandon epistemology and take up the history of philosophy (even though he in fact has no interest in doing so).[6]

We do not, therefore, normally hold that the only project or career a person is permitted to follow is the one he is in fact following or interested in following, or that a person's permission to choose some career is conditional on his actually having chosen or being interested in it. Yet the usual accounts of what makes it permissible for an agent, despite the contrary dictates of utilitarianism, to pursue a non-optimific personal project entail only a permission to pursue the particular career an agent is interested in and cannot account for his permission to choose and pursue whatever career or project he wants. They can account, if he is interested in epistemology, for his justification in pursuing that career and can explain why act-utilitarianism is wrong to deny him that justification. But, given that very interest, they fail to account for that fact that it is also (still) morally permissible for him to go into the history of philosophy and any number of other areas (we would ordinarily say he has such moral freedom even if it isn't going to – indeed can't – take full advantage of it). For notice that to deny him such permissions – such freedom – is not, given his actual personality, to demand any sacrifice or threaten his 'integrity'; so this sort of common-sense permission cannot be defended on grounds of integrity, etc., and if we want a justification for all the permissions to pursue projects that common-sense grants but utilitarianism denies us, we need something more general, something that accounts for more than our permission to pursue the particular project(s) we are actually committed to.

It would appear, then, that although common-sense grants us a moral freedom to pursue careers and projects other than those we actually have chosen or actually will choose, considerations of integrity or undue demandingness are only relevant to our freedom to pursue the particular projects we are committed to; and thus fail to account for our full moral freedom with regard to projects, life plans, careers and commitments. In order to justify and explain our permissions regarding careers other than those we actually do choose, I think, in fact, that we need some account of why we are morally permitted or free to choose and pursue *any (innocent) project whatever* (quite independently of whether we ever are or will be actually interested in pursuing it).

But there are possible misunderstandings here. I have distinguished between a broader freedom or permission to pursue whatever (innocent) project one wants (or wishes or chooses), and the narrower permission to pursue the particular project one actually does choose to follow, but the distinction can easily be blurred or obscured if we misunderstand the 'logic' of that broader permission. If we understand the permission to pursue whatever project one chooses as involving, with regard to all projects x, a permission to pursue x if one chooses to pursue x, and understand the latter 'if' as involving a (material) conditional of some sort, then the permission, say, to pursue the history of philosophy will have to be understood as a permission conditional upon the actual choice (or wish or desire) to pursue that project. Such a conditional permission is all that arguments from integrity, etc., allow one to account for, but it is less than the blanket permission (common-sense grants us) to pursue whatever project one wants. Long ago J. L. Austin pointed out a use of 'if' that is non-conditional, and gave us such memorable examples as 'there are biscuits on the sideboard if you want them' and (thanks to Geach) 'I paid you back yesterday, if you remember' and, of course, 'I can if I choose'.[7] 'There are biscuits on the sideboard if you want them' does not make the presence of biscuits conditional in any way on one's wanting them. And by the same token the moralist who says you may pursue epistemology if you wish is not making your permission to pursue epistemology in any way conditional on your actually wishing (now or ever) to pursue that particular career. He is simply saying: you may pursue epistemology (whether or not you actually wish to do so).

Now Austin pointed out the existence of non-conditional 'ifs', but given the connection between 'ifs' and quantification, we should not be surprised to find ordinary language universal quantifications involving a *tacit* non-conditional 'if', and this is precisely what is involved in asserting a universal permission to pursue any (innocent) project one wants.[8] This is not merely to grant with regard to any x, a permission to pursue x conditional upon one's actually wanting x.[9] Rather, the permission to pursue whatever project one wishes (wants), the permission to pursue any innocent project if one chooses, is simply the blanket permission to pursue any innocent project, the permission, with regard to any possible project x, to pursue x.[10] And this is not a narrow permission to pursue the project one has in fact chosen; it is a permission in no way conditional upon the assumption that the project(s) permitted has (have) actually been chosen.

It should now be clear that the permission granted by ordinary morality in connection with projects, careers, life plans, and commitments are not as limited as recent discussions suggest. From the common-sense standpoint we do not merely possess the permission to pursue the particular project we have in fact chosen or will choose, but have the broader moral permission or moral freedom to pursue any (innocent) project whatever, and this blanket permission antedates our choice of particular career and survives it, so that subsequent to that choice, we still retain the moral permission to pursue projects other than those actually chosen. Given our ordinary moral assumptions, a person who has just chosen a long-range project in epistemology retains the moral freedom to pursue a career in painting or history of philosophy. And this is simply a consequence of the fact that our common-sense permissions to pursue careers are not conditional on any choice of or commitment to projects or careers but seem, instead, to be a function of our morally permitted *autonomy* in choosing careers.

Assuming, then, that we have no option, from a common-sense standpoint, but to acknowledge a wider class of project-related (and commitment-related) permissions, the issue of how we should justify or explain these permissions naturally arises. Should we, for example, divide this wider class into permissions pertaining to actually chosen projects and permissions pertaining to merely possible projects and say that explanations in terms of integrity or what counts as unreasonable sacrifice give the fundamental rationale for the first group but that another explanation (other explanations) must be sought for the second? I think not. For consider the person who has chosen a project in epistemology. If we take his or her permission to pursue that project to be based ultimately on the hardship or disintegrational alienating effects of *abandoning* that project, then we indeed take that permission to be conditional upon the fact that the person in question is actually committed to epistemology, rather than as a permission that antedates and is independent of that particular choice. And this seems very odd. Why should one's permission to be an epistemologist have a different ultimate source from one's permission to be a painter just because one has in fact chosen to be an epistemologist? It seems more plausible to hold, instead, that all permissions to pursue (possible) projects are of a piece, that they are all, ultimately, of the same *moral kind*. It is natural, in other words, to group all these permissions together, rather than claim that one subclass has a quite different source from the remainder. Let us assume, then, that for the person interested in epistemology, the permission to pursue projects in that area is of a piece with a large number of other permissions relating to different possible careers, and is simply that particular permission out of that large class which the person in question has chosen to act upon. His moral permission to work on the particular project he is interested in can then be treated simply as an *instance* of his (our) general moral freedom to choose and pursue any (innocent) project whatever. (We can then also avoid having to say that the respective permissions to pursue epistemology possessed by two individuals, one who has chosen epistemology and the other history of philosophy, have different bases, or that a single individual's permission to do epistemology has one basis rather than another depending on whether he in fact goes in for epistemology.)

Moreover, we can regard all our project-related permissions as constituting a single moral kind without denying all force to the rationale of integrity or of undue sacrifice. For even if these latter cannot provide the fundamental justification for project-related permissions, still someone who has chosen a particular career may have an additional and independent justification for following it that he would not have if he were not committed to it (and that others not committed to it may lack) in terms, e.g., of the sacrifice that giving it up would entail for him in particular. But still, if they constitute a single moral kind, our permissions – assuming they exist – to pursue (actual and possible) projects cannot basically be justified in terms of integrity or considerations of what counts as undue sacrifice, but must have another underlying rationale, and, as I have already briefly suggested, I think this rationale may lie in the idea of individual autonomy. Given our ordinary understanding of the notion, an individual has (*de facto*) autonomy in a given sphere, if he has the power to do whatever he chooses within that sphere, a power conceived not as the power to do the thing he in fact chooses or will choose, as a power conditional upon choice, but rather as a power to do anything whatever in the relevant sphere.[11] Such autonomy is precisely analogous to the blanket permission to pursue whatever innocent project one chooses that common-sense morality seems to grant us, and it is indeed natural to characterize our moral permission to pursue any (innocent) project whatever as a kind (form) of *moral autonomy*. The appealing idea of individual autonomy can then be seen as providing the underlying rationale for that broad class of project-related and commitment-related permissions that common-sense grants and utilitarianism denies.[12]

There is, of course, something intuitively appealing in the idea that moral injunctions should not alienate the individual from his deepest held commitments and also in the idea that moral codes should not be unduly demanding, but as we have seen, these ideas do not allow one to justify, against utilitarian or consequentialist encroachment, the entire range of our common-sense permissions to pursue projects and commitments. Their focus is simply too narrow. On the other hand, the (ordinary) idea of autonomy not only has common-sense appeal, but, unlike these other considera-

31

tions, can be used to support the full range of common-sense permissions to pursue projects. Our moral permission to choose any innocent project or commitment whatever is naturally thought of as deriving from and expressing a reasonable and appealing ideal of individual autonomy.

The concept of autonomy thus organizes and focuses the thinking of those who assert a blanket common-sense permission to pursue any innocent project whatever; it constitutes (a major part of) the appeal and the presumptive justification for the full range of common-sense project-related permissions that common-sense affirms and act-consequentialism denies, and as a single natural rubric, it also allows us to treat the class of these permissions as the moral kind it appears to be. The notion of autonomy also enables us properly to identify the locus of disagreement between common-sense morality and consequentialism as regards these permissions. For to speak of integrity or undue self-sacrifice is to leave out of account those permissions concerning the merely possible that common-sense grants and consequentialism denies, and thus to fail to account for a major part of the disagreement between these two, for a major part of the complaint that common-sense has against consequentialism in this area. But if what has been said above is correct, that complaint can be adequately (though briefly) expressed in the charge that act-consequentialism unreasonably infringes (or fails to respect) the autonomy of individuals.

An emphasis on autonomy not only helps to provide a unified account of the justification or appeal of the full range of common-sense permissions to pursue projects (and commitments), but also enables us to treat 'agent-sacrificing' permissions as of a piece with project-related permissions rather than as weird and *sui generis*. We saw that agent-sacrificing permissions cannot be accounted for in terms of integrity or considerations of unreasonable self-sacrifice, but the notion of autonomy does subsume these permissions. Our moral autonomy includes the permission to pursue projects regarding which we have no interest as well as those in which we do take an interest; and the idea of autonomy involves our freedom to choose or not choose projects quite independently of those very decisions or choices, quite independently of our actual interest or commitment. But the permission to ignore one's own good or prefer another's greater to one's own lesser good (even when one in fact lacks an interest in doing these things) also seems to fall under the idea of individual autonomy. If in the name of autonomy one can claim that a person has permissions to pursue projects he in fact has no interest in pursuing, it does not seem inappropriate to ground the permission to favour others or neglect oneself in a similar appeal. For if autonomy is to have any meaning it must signify a power or permission to do more than (things other than) the things one actually desires (or that are actually in one's own interest) and it seems to me that whether this involves pursuing projects one has no actual interest in or failing to pursue benefits that one *is* interested in, these permissions can be seen as falling under, and gaining some of their appeal from, the idea of autonomy.

Moreover, when I originally mentioned agent-sacrificing permissions, those permissions seemed odd, and possibly dismissible, because they involved permission to sacrifice one's own (greater) good even when one actually lacks desire to do so. But once we notice that even some of our permissions regarding projects involve permissions vis-à-vis projects we are not in fact interested in, the idea of permissions for undesired or unintended actions, rather than seeming odd, turns out to follow from the very idea of autonomy. [By the same token, ethical egoism in an important sense opposes our autonomy by demanding that we *not* be indifferent to our own good or prefer others' good to our own (greater) good.] So the idea of autonomy allows us to account for agent-sacrificing permissions, and by treating them as of a piece with all other common-sense permissions, to draw the sting of oddness from them.

The emphasis on autonomy thus helps to consolidate our understanding of common-sense moral permissions (indeed of common-sense morality in general) in a way that appeals to integrity or undue sacrifice are simply incapable of doing.[13] Of course, to say that all common-sense permissions can be understood as falling under the rubric of autonomy is not necessarily to have undermined act-utilitarianism. There is something independently appealing in the notion of autonomy invoked above, and by showing that different-seeming common-sense permissions all fall under that single appealing rubric some new support for these permissions is generated. But act-consequentialism has its own independent sources of appeal, and the previous discussion hardly represents a knock-down argument against consequentialism or a proof of common-sense morality. On the other hand, our emphasis on autonomy does do something to clarify where the disagreement between consequentialism and common-sense morality actually lies and also gives a more unified and general explanation than has been offered elsewhere of the source and rationale of the whole set of common-sense permissions that act-consequentialism denies.[14]

III

SATISFICING CONSEQUENTIALISM

In the present chapter, I would like to discuss a version of consequentialism which is not only of considerable interest in its own right, but may also help to answer or at least mitigate the common-sense criticism, introduced in Chapter II, that act-consequentialism infringes the moral autonomy of agents.

Act-consequentialism is generally characterized as a certain sort of view about the relation between an act's rightness and its consequences. An act-consequentialist holds that states of affairs (outcomes, consequences) can be objectively or impersonally ranked according to their goodness and that any given act is morally right or permissible if and only if its consequences are at least as good, according to the impersonal ranking, as those of any alternative act open to the agent – the doing of an act being itself included among its consequences.[1] An act-utilitarian is, according to the prevalent conception, an act-consequentialist with a particular view about how states of affairs, or consequences, are to be impersonally ranked: roughly speaking, the goodness of states of affairs depends only on the well-being, happiness, satisfaction, utility, or desire-fulfilment of the individuals who exist in those states of affairs and one state of affairs is better than another just in case it contains a greater sum of individual utilities, or a greater overall balance of satisfaction over dissatisfaction.[2] Thus act-consequentialism holds that a right act must be optimific, and the act-utilitarian, in addition, that optimizing always means *maximizing* the sum of individual well-being, desire-fulfilment, etc. But these theses need not go together. Nowadays,

35

it is by no means unusual for an (act-)consequentialist not to be a utilitarian and to hold, for example, that considerations of justice may affect the goodness of overall states of affairs without affecting the sum total of individual utilities.

Act-consequentialism itself, on the other hand, has been seen as a unitary moral conception by both defenders and critics. But the claim that the rightness of an act depends on whether it produces the best consequences impersonally judged can in fact be broken down into a pair of claims that need not go together, and the major purpose of the present chapter will be to show how this is possible and, in consequence, to suggest a useful widening of the notion of (act-)consequentialism. The idea that the rightness of an act depends solely on its consequences, i.e., on how (impersonally) good its consequences are, is separable from the idea that the rightness of an act depends on its having the best consequences (producible in the circumstances); the second of these theses entails the first, but not vice versa, yet standard conceptions of consequentialism entail both these theses. Roughly, then, consequentialism standardly involves the claim that the rightness of acts depends on whether their consequences are good enough together with the particular view that only the best possible (in certain circumstances) is good enough. And given this way of partitioning standard consequentialism, it is not perhaps immediately obvious why these two theses should naturally or inevitably go together. Could not someone who held that rightness depended solely on how good an act's consequences were also want to hold that less than the best was sometimes good enough, hold, in other words, that an act might qualify as morally right through having good enough consequences, even though better consequences could have been produced in the circumstances?

In what follows I shall try to give some of the reasons why someone might want to hold just this sort of view. It is a view that, to the best of my knowledge, has not been explicitly suggested previously; but I hope to show not only that there is nothing incoherent about it but also that it has attractive features lacking in standard act-consequentialism. Furthermore, it seems terminologically natural to treat any view that makes rightness depend solely on the goodness of consequences as a form of consequentialism, so once the feasibility of the idea that less than the best may be good enough becomes apparent, it will be appropriate to treat

36

the view that rightness depends on whether consequences are good enough and that less than the best may sometimes be good enough as a form of consequentialism. The traditional or standard view that rightness depends on whether the consequences are the best producible in the circumstances will then most naturally be seen as a particular kind of consequentialism, rather than as constituting consequentialism *per se*.[3] And it will be natural to characterize this particular kind of consequentialism as 'optimizing consequentialism' since it holds that rightness depends on whether consequences are good enough and that only the best is good enough. By contrast, the new sort of consequentialist view just mentioned might appropriately be labelled 'satisficing consequentialism', if we may borrow from the recent literature of economics, where the notion of satisficing has been used to express the idea that (rational) economic agents may sometimes seek less than the best, may sometimes choose what is good enough, without regard for whether what they have chosen is the best thing (outcome) available in the circumstances.

Now the idea of satisficing consequentialism (and the obviously consequent idea of satisficing utilitarianism) deserves to be explored as a formal possibility quite apart from its intuitiveness or ultimate supportability; but in fact it can be made to appear of more than formal interest. Even those opposed to consequentialism and utilitarianism as moral theories have tended to think that (extramoral individualistic) rationality requires an individual to maximize his satisfactions or do what is best for himself;[4] but the recent economics literature concerning satisficing suggests the possibility of a non-optimizing form of individual rational choice, and by giving a brief philosophical elaboration of the idea of rational satisficing, I hope to make the idea of *moral* satisficing, and satisficing consequentialism in particular, seem more attractive. It will turn out, furthermore, that ordinary or common-sense morality also regards acts that are less than the best (most beneficent) possible as sometimes good enough (beneficent enough) and so not morally wrong even apart from any sacrifices a better (more beneficent) act might require from the agent. And to the degree that common-sense morality allows for 'moral satisficing' in the area of beneficence (benevolence), the possibility of a satisficing form of (utilitarian) consequentialism is also underscored and made more appealing. After all, consequentialists have long sought for ways – rule utilitarianism, probabilistic act-utilitarianism, etc. – of reconciling their views (making them seem less out of line) with common-sense morality, and we shall see towards the end of this chapter, that satisficing consequentialism has a number of advantages, in terms of common-sense moral plausibility, over optimizing forms of consequentialism, utilitarian and non-utilitarian alike. We shall also see that prominent views about the object of and motivation behind morality that are taken to support optimizing consequentialism or utilitarianism support these views only in their most general form and are equally consistent with optimizing or satisficing versions. But first to the idea of rational individual satisficing.

1

Consider an example borrowed from the satisficing literature of economics, but treated in such a way as to emphasize its relevance to philosophical discussions of rationality, rather than its implications for economic theory.[5] An individual planning to move to a new location and having to sell his house may seek, not to maximize his profit on the house, not to get the best price for it he is likely to receive within some appropriate time period, but simply to obtain what he takes to be a good or satisfactory price. What he deems satisfactory may depend, among other things, on what he paid for the house, what houses cost in the place where he is relocating, and on what houses like his normally sell at. But given some notion of what would be a good or satisfactory price to sell at, he may fix the price of his house at that point, rather than attempting, by setting it somewhat higher, to do better than that, or do the best he can. His reason for not setting the price higher will not, in that case, be some sort of anxiety about not being able to sell the house at all or some feeling that trying to do better would likely not be worth the effort of figuring out how to get the best price possible (or a better price). Nor is he so rich that any extra money he received for the house would be practically meaningless in terms of marginal utility. Rather he is a 'satisficer' content with good enough and does not seek to maximize (optimize) his expectations. His desires, his needs, are moderate, and perhaps knowing this about himself, he may not be particularly interested in doing better for himself than he is likely to do by selling at a merely satisfactory price. If someone pointed out that it would be better for him to get more money, he would reply, not by disagreeing, but by pointing out that for him at least a good enough price is good enough.

Such a person clearly fails to exemplify the maximizing and optimizing model of individual rationality advocated by utilitarians like Sidgwick and anti-utilitarians like Rawls. But I think he none-theless represents a possible idea of (one kind of) individual rationality, and the literature of economic satisficing in the main treats such examples, both as regards individuals and as regards economic units like the firm or offices of centralized state planning, as exemplifying a form of reasonable or rational behaviour. It might be possible to hold on to an optimizing or maximizing model of rationality and regard satisficing examples as indications of the enormous prevalence of irrational human behaviour, but this has typically not been done by economists, and I think philosophers would have even less reason to do so. For there are many other cases where satisficing seems rational, or at least not irrational, and although some of these are purely hypothetical, hypothetical examples are the stock-in-trade of ethical and moral-psychological theory even when they are of little or no interest to economists.

Imagine that it is mid-afternoon; you had a good lunch, and you are not now hungry; neither, on the other hand, are you sated. You would enjoy a candy bar or Coca Cola, if you had one, and there is in fact, right next to your desk, a refrigerator stocked with such snacks and provided gratis by the company for which you work. Realizing all this, do you, then, necessarily take and consume a snack? If you do not, is that necessarily because you are afraid to spoil your dinner, because you are on a diet or because you are too busy? I think not. You may simply not feel the need for any such snack. You turn down a good thing, a sure satisfaction, because you are perfectly satisfied as you are. Most of us are often in situations of this sort, and many of us would often do the same thing. We are not boundless optimizers or maximizers, but are sometimes (more) modest in our desires and needs. But such modesty, such moderation, need not be irrational or unreasonable on our part.

Of course moderation has been exalted as a prime virtue in

many religious and philosophical traditions. But when, for example, the Epicureans emphasized the rationality of moderation in the pursuit of pleasure, they recommended modesty in one's desires only as a means to an overall more pleasurable life, and in the example mentioned above, moderation is not functioning as a means to greater overall satisfactions. One is not worried about ruining one's dinner or one's figure, and the moderation exemplified is thus quite different from the instrumental virtue recommended by the Epicureans. The sort of moderation I am talking about, then, is not for the sake of anything else, indeed it may not be for its own sake either, if by that is meant that it is some sort of admirable trait or virtue. If one has the habit of not trying to eke out the last possible satisfaction from situations and of resting content with some reasonable quantity that is less than the most or best one can do, then one has a habit of moderation or modesty as regards one's desires and satisfactions, and it may not be irrational or stupid to have such a habit, even if (one recognizes that) the contrary habit of maximizing may also represent something neither irrational nor stupid. But if a maximizer (optimizer) lacking the habit of moderation in the above sense need not be immoderate in that ordinary sense of the term that implies unreasonableness, then the habit of being satisfied with less than the most or best may not be a virtue, even if such moderation, such modesty is also neither irrational nor an anti-virtue.[6]

But if there is (were) nothing irrational or unreasonable about maximizing, isn't the moderate individual who is content with less a kind of ascetic? Not necessarily. An ascetic is someone who, within certain limits, minimizes his enjoyments or satisfactions; he deliberately leaves himself with less, unsatisfied. The moderate individual, on the other hand, is someone content with (what he considers) a reasonable amount of satisfaction; he wants to be satisfied and up to a certain point he wants more satisfactions rather than fewer, to be better off rather than worse off; but there is a point beyond which he has no desire, and even refuses, to go. There is a space between asceticism and the attempt to maximize satisfactions, do the best one can for oneself, a space occupied by the habit (if not the virtue) of moderation. And because such moderation is not a form of asceticism, it is difficult to see why it should count as irrational from the standpoint of egoistic or extramoral individual rationality.[7]

Now the kind of example just mentioned differs from the case of satisficing house selling in being independent of any monetary transaction. It is more privatistic or purely philosophical than the examples that appear in the economics literature of satisficing. But the example differs importantly in another way from those economics examples. Economists who have advocated the model of rational satisficing for individuals, firms, or state bodies have stressed the need for or appropriateness of such behaviour with regard to real-life choices which, through the complexity of the circumstances in which they occur, may be beyond the reach of maximizing or optimizing techniques. In cases of decision under less than total knowledge, an entrepreneur or firm may simply seek a satisfactory return on investment, a satisfactory share of the market, a satisfactory level of sales, rather than attempting to maximize or optimize under any of these headings. And his reason may have nothing to do with the costs of trying to do better, e.g., the costs of gaining further information or effecting some new policy. Like the home-seller of our earlier example, an entre- preneur may simply, for example, be satisfied with a certain profit and give no thought to trying to do better. But this idea of rational satisficing implies only that individuals or firms *do not* always *seek* to maximize or optimize and are *satisfied* with attaining a certain 'aspiration level' less than the best that might be envisaged. It does not imply that it could be rational actually to *reject* the better for the good enough in situations where both were available. In the example of house selling, the individual accepts less than he might well be able to get, but he doesn't accept a lower price when a higher bidder makes an equally firm offer. And writers on satisficing generally seem to hold that satisficing only makes sense as a habit of not seeking what is better or best, rather than as a habit of actually rejecting the better, when it is clearly available, for the good enough. Thus Herbert Simon, in one of the classics of the satisficing literature, develops the idea of aspiration level and of satisficing, but goes on to say that 'when a firm has alternatives open to it that are at or above its aspiration level, it will choose the best of those known to be available.'[8]

However, the example of not taking the afternoon snack challenges the idea that the satisficing individual will never explicitly reject the better for the good enough. For the individual in question turns down an immediately available satisfaction, something he knows he will enjoy. He isn't merely not trying for a maximum of satisfactions, but is explicitly rejecting such a maximum. (It may be easier to see the explicitness of the rejection if we change the example so that he is actually offered a snack by someone and replies: no thank you, I'm just fine as I am.) And I think that most of us would argue that there is nothing irrational here. Many of us, most of us, occasionally reject afternoon snacks, second cups of tea, etc., not out of (unconscious) asceticism, not because we are irrational about satisfactions, but because (to some degree) we have a habit of moderation with regard to certain needs or satisfactions. The hypothetical example of the afternoon snack thus takes the idea of rational satisficing a step beyond where economists, to the best of my knowledge, have been willing to go; but such a step should nonetheless have some philosophical appeal in the light of the moral/psychological example of moderation in desires mentioned above.

At this point, however, it may be objected that the example may be one of rational behaviour, or rational non-behaviour, but is less than clear as an example of satisficing. The individual in question prefers not to have a certain satisfaction and certainly he deliberately rejects the maximization of satisfactions, if we think of satisfactions as like pleasures or enjoyments. (The individual may or may not feel some satisfaction *at* having satisficed, and in particular at the fact that he has enough and needs nothing better than what he has in order to be satisfied, but presumably he is not aiming at this second-order pleasure or satisfaction; it is a by-product of turning down a certain satisfaction or pleasure.) But to the extent the individual rejects an available satisfaction, he presumably shows himself to prefer (or desire) not to have that satisfaction and so in some (trivial?) sense is maximizing the satisfaction of his preferences (or desires).[9] More importantly, perhaps, it is not clear that the moderate individual must think of himself as missing out on anything *good* when he forgoes the afternoon snack. For although he knows he would enjoy the snack, the very fact that he rejects such enjoyment might easily be taken as evidence that he doesn't in the circumstances regard such enjoyment as a good thing. In that case, he may be satisficing in terms of some quantitative notion of satisfaction, but not with respect to some more refined or flexible notion of (his own) individual good, and the example would only provide a counter-example to a rather crude maximizing ideal of rationality, not to the idea that it is irrational (egoistically or individualistically) to choose what is less good for one when something better is available.

However, even if the enjoyment of a snack does count as a rejected personal good for the individual of our example, that fact may be obscured by the very smallness or triviality of the good in question. It may be very difficult even for the individual himself to know (have any definite views as to) whether, in rejecting the opportunity for a snack, he is turning down a good thing because he feels that what he already has is good enough or, instead, is regarding the enjoyment of a snack as not a good thing in those circumstances. In order to deal with such doubts, it may, then, be advisable to consider other examples, more purely hypothetical than the present one, where the good forgone through satisficing is 'writ large' and fairly obvious even to the satisficing agent.

How do we react to fairy tales in which the hero or heroine, offered a single wish, asks for and receives something very good or desirable? He may wish, for example, for a pot of gold, or a casket of jewels or a million (1900) dollars, or, simply, for (enough money to enable) his family and himself to be comfortably well off for the rest of their lives. In each case the person asks for less than he might have asked for, but we are not typically struck by the thought that he was *irrational* to ask for less than he could have, and neither, in general, do the fairy tales themselves imply a criticism of this sort; so, given the tendency of such tales to be full of moralism about human folly, we have, I think, some evidence that such fairy-tale wishes need not be regarded as irrational. (In not regarding them as irrational, we need not confuse what we know *about* fairy tales with what the individual *in* a given fairy tale ought to know. In some fairy tales, people who ask for too much fail to get their wish or have it realized in an unacceptable way. But there is no reason to suppose that we consider the person who in a given fairy tale asks for enough to be comfortable not to be irrational only because we mistakenly imagine him to have some evidence concerning the possible risks of asking for more than he does.)[10]

43

Now the individual in the fairy tale who wishes for *less* than he could presumably exemplifies the sort of moderation discussed earlier. He may think that a pot of gold or enough money to live comfortably is all he needs to be satisfied, that anything more is of no particular importance to him. (Surely such a wish is not indicative of asceticism.) At the same time, however, he may realize (be willing to admit) that he could do better for himself by asking for more. He needn't imagine himself constitutionally incapable of benefiting from additional money or gold, for the idea that one will be happy, or satisfied, with a certain level of existence by no means precludes the thought (though it perhaps precludes *dwelling* on the thought)[11] that one will not be as well off as one possibly could be. It merely precludes the sense of wanting or needing more for oneself, and of being dissatisfied. Indeed the very fact that someone could actually explicitly wish for enough money to be comfortably well-off is itself sufficient evidence of what I am saying. Someone who makes such a wish clearly acknowledges the possibility of being better off and yet chooses – knowingly and in some sense deliberately chooses – a lesser but personally satisfying degree of well-being. And it is precisely because the stakes are so large in such cases of wishing that they provide clearcut examples of presumably rational individual satisficing. But, again, the sort of satisficing involved is not (merely) the kind familiar in the economics literature where (because of the complexity of circumstances) an individual seeks something other than optimum results, but a kind of satisficing that actually rejects the available better for the available good enough. Although the individual with the wish would be better off if he wished for more, he asks for less (we may suppose that if the wish grantor prods him by asking 'Are you sure you wouldn't like more money than that?', he sticks with his original request). And if we have any sympathy with the idea of moderation, of modesty, in one's desires, we shall have to grant that the satisficing individual who wishes, e.g., for less money is not irrational. Perhaps we ourselves would not be so easily satisfied in his circumstances, but that needn't make us think him irrational for being moderate in a way, or to a degree, that we are not.[12]

Given the above discussion of the nature and justification of rational satisficing, the way may be prepared for an examination of moral satisficing. But I shall not immediately proceed to a discussion of (the varieties of) satisficing consequentialism, because I believe we can make the strongest case for this new form of consequentialism by first pointing out the non-optimizing character of the common-sense morality of benevolence (beneficence).

Consider a manager of a resort hotel who discovers, late one evening, that a car has broken down right outside her premises. In the car are a poor family of four who haven't the money to rent a cabin or buy a meal at the hotel, but the manager has the power and authority to offer them a cabin gratis, and she in fact decides to do so, assuming (as we may assume for the sake of argument) that it would be wrong of her not to do so. In acting thus benevolently, however, she doesn't go through the complete list of all the empty cabins in order to put them in the best cabin available. She simply goes through the list of cabins till she finds a cabin in good repair that is large enough to suit the family. Imagine, further, that, as with examples of rational satisficing from the economics literature, she chooses the cabin she does because it seems a satisfactory choice, good enough, not because, as an optimizer, she thinks that further search through the list of cabins will not be worth it in terms of time expended and the likelihood of finding a (sufficiently) better cabin. In such circumstances, optimizing act-consequentialism or act-utilitarianism would presumably hold that the manager should look further for a better room. (Assume there is a better room and that she will easily find it if she proceeds further through the list.) But I think ordinary morality would regard her actions as benevolent and her choice of a particular room for the family in question as morally acceptable, not wrong. She may not display the optimizing benevolence that standard act-consequentialism would require, under the circumstances, but in ordinary moral terms she has done well enough by the family that is stranded and had no obligation to do any better.

The example illustrates the possibility of a morally acceptable satisficing benevolence that does not seek to optimize with respect to those benefited (or those affected) by one's actions. But our earlier examples of rational individual satisficing extended the notion beyond the usual examples from the literature of economics to include cases where someone explicitly rejects a better (or the best) alternative; and the same possibility in fact also exists in the area of moral satisficing. Thus consider again our hotel manager and the travellers she benefits. They have now moved into the cabin she has found for them, and they are all hungry. But it is late; so the manager tells the lone remaining waiter in the restaurant to bring out a meal for the travellers from among the dishes that remain from dinner and that will not be usable the next day. Assume that there are a large variety of dishes, some more luxurious or splendid than others, and that the waiter asks what, among these things, he should bring the newly arrived travellers. The hotel manager may say: oh, just something good and substantial, it needn't be too fancy or elaborate. Alternatively, the waiter may ask whether he should bring them the 'special dinner' and the manager may say: no, there's no need for anything that fancy, just bring them something appetizing and good. In either case, the manager seems deliberately to be rejecting an alternative that stands a good chance of being preferable to the poor family in question. Most people (let us assume) prefer the 'special dinner', apart from its price, and the manager has no reason to believe that her new guests are particularly moderate or modest in their desires. Yet her reason for choosing as she does may not be consideration for the waiter, who may have the same amount of work to do whatever he brings the family to eat, nor even less a snobbish sense of charity that regards the 'special dinner' as too good for the family in question. Rather, she may be expressing in her benevolent actions a kind of moderation that she may also evince in her self-regarding choices. And, again, I think common-sense would regard such deliberately non-optimific benevolence as morally acceptable, not wrong.

In addition, if I may appeal again to an even more hypothetical example, in order to underscore the similarity with what was said earlier about self-regarding individual rationality, consider a fairy-tale wish regarding people other than oneself. A warrior has fought meritoriously and died in a good cause, and the gods wish to grant him a single wish for those he leaves behind, before he enters Paradise and ceases to be concerned with his previous life. Presented with such an opportunity, may not the warrior wish for *his family* to be comfortably well off forever after? And will we from a common-sense standpoint consider him to have acted wrongly or non-benevolently towards his family because he (presumably knowingly) rejected an expectably better lot for them in favour of what was simply good enough? Surely not.

But the warrior and hotel manager examples not only offer further illustration of the idea of satisficing benevolence, but also help to make clear that common-sense morality differs from standard optimizing consequentialism with regard to the morality of benevolence quite apart from issues concerning the amount of sacrifice one may correctly require from moral agents (or concerning the proper autonomy of such agents). In the fairy-tale example of the dying warrior, the warrior who chooses less than the (possible or likely) best for his family does not do so because a choice of something better would require too great a sacrifice. Neither choice would require *any* sort of personal sacrifice. And by the same token the hotel manager's personal sacrifice (if any) presumably stays constant however splendid a meal she decides to give the poor travellers. So the divergence between common-sense morality and standard act-consequentialism and act-utilitarianism with regard to such cases cannot be accounted for in terms of a disagreement over whether one can correctly require an agent to sacrifice his own desires, projects and concerns in the name of overall optimality. With regard to such cases they disagree, rather, as to how much good an agent may be morally required to do (for others) given a total absence, or constant amount, of agent sacrifice. Optimizing act-utilitarianism and act-consequentialism will hold that the moral agent must produce the most good possible (the best possible results) in such circumstances, ordinary morality that producing a sufficient non-optimal amount of good (sufficiently good non-optimal results) may be all that is required.

Of course, this is hardly the only, or even the most important, way in which common-sense morality diverges from optimizing act-consequentialism: as we have seen, ordinary morality also contains deontological restrictions or side-constraints on what an agent may permissibly do in the name of overall optimality. But the fact that common-sense morality allows a satisficing concern for good results, a less than optimific beneficence, to be permissible in some cases where deontological restrictions are irrelevant (and where there is no issue of personal sacrifice on the part of the agent) suggests the possibility of a satisficing form of pure (act-) consequentialism. And since the plausibility of various forms of consequentialism partly depends on how far their implications diverge from the deliverances of ordinary moral intuition, this new form of consequentialism may turn out to have some distinctive advantages over traditional optimizing forms of consequentialism.

The idea of satisficing act-consequentialism is not, in fact, entirely new. It is to a certain extent anticipated, for example, by the sort of 'negative utilitarianism', proposed briefly by Karl Popper in *The Open Society and its Enemies*, according to which we have a moral duty to minimize suffering and evil, but no general duty to maximize human happiness.[13] In the course of defending this doctrine, Popper claims, in particular, that the idea of relieving suffering has a greater moral appeal to us than the idea of increasing the happiness of a man who is doing well already. So Popper not only offers an example of non-optimizing consequentialism, but indicates that it can be based on 'satisficing' common-sense moral intuitions of the kind we ourselves mentioned above.[14]

But Popper suggests only one form of non-optimizing consequentialism, and it is a form attended by a number of serious difficulties. The fact, assuming it is a fact, that adding to happiness has less moral appeal than relieving suffering hardly implies, for example, that our only duty is to relieve suffering. And the latter idea, which constitutes the essence of negative utilitarianism, seems to have the absurd consequence that we would do all that duty requires, if we painlessly destroyed all of suffering humanity (sentient life).[15] Negative utilitarianism seems, then, to entail unacceptable views about when less than the best possible is good enough. But by virtue of its asymmetric treatment of human happiness and suffering it also rules out the possibility of morally permissible satisficing throughout a wide range of cases. Wherever the relief of suffering is in question, it demands that suffering be minimized; but common-sense morality is not in fact so demanding in this respect. A medic attending the wounded on the battlefield may attend to the first (sufficiently) badly wounded person he sees without considering whether there may be someone in even worse shape nearby, and from a common-sense moral standpoint such behaviour seems perfectly acceptable. So although Popper's variety of satisficing consequentialism involves a fundamental asymmetry between good and evil, happiness and suffering, a less asymmetric form of such consequentialism may, for a number of reasons, be more attractive and intuitive. What was appealing, in our discussion of rational individual satisficing, was the idea of a reasonable sufficiency of good less than the best attainable. But this idea gains only imperfect expression in a moral theory like negative utilitarianism, which, among other things, treats the eradication of our suffering race as 'good enough' but not the behaviour of the morally satisficing medic. What may be needed is a form of satisficing consequentialism with a more plausible conception of what counts as good enough, and it will help us towards such a theory, if we consider another form of satisficing consequentialism that can be found in one of the great classics of utilitarian moral philosophy, Bentham's *An Introduction to the Principles of Morals and Legislation*.

The 1823 edition of the *Introduction* differs from that published in 1789 principally in regard to some clarificatory notes, and one of these notes discusses the Principle of Utility and interprets it as requiring that everyone seek the greatest happiness of those affected by his actions. But the unaltered main text of the book treats the Principle of Utility in quite a different (indeed incompatible) way as 'that principle which approves or disapproves of every action whatsoever, according to the tendency which it appears to have to augment or diminish the happiness of the party whose interest is in question: or, what is the same thing in other words, to promote or to oppose that happiness.'[16] The discussion in the footnote presents a typical optimizing form of act-consequentialism and act utilitarianism; but the earlier main text says nothing about 'best' or 'greatest good'. An act is said to be right if it tends to augment or promote happiness, wrong if it has the opposite effect, and since an act may promote happiness without producing the most happiness possible, in given circumstances, the earlier text presents a kind of satisficing utilitarian act-consequentialism. (As with Popper's discussion, a particular form of satisficing consequentialism is advocated without the *general idea* of satisficing (act-)consequentialism or (act-)utilitarianism being mentioned. Perhaps that is why Bentham also fails to mention the incompatibility between the two kinds of act-utilitarianism he offers.)

Now the form of satisficing consequentialism Bentham advocates has some peculiar features, features that must be avoided if we are to arrive at a fully satisfying version of such consequentialism. If we take it quite literally, his theory treats the rightness of any action as dependent solely on the results of that single action. No comparison to the results of available alternative actions is either necessary or relevant. On Bentham's (satisficing) view, an act is right if it adds very little to the sum of human happiness (the net balance of happiness over unhappiness) and even if an alternative is available which is much more productive of happiness. By the same token, an act is wrong if it subtracts from the sum of human happiness, even when every available alternative has worse results. (Given typical utilitarian notions of consequences and results, it is easy to imagine such cases.) These implications do not square with ordinary moral intuitions, and they are due to the *non-comparativeness* of the just-mentioned form of consequentialism. Bentham's satisficing consequentialism regards an act as having produced *enough* good or happiness to be right if it favourably alters the balance of happiness over unhappiness even to the *slightest* extent, but if an alternative is available which would produce much more good, we should perhaps not normally feel that a slight addition to happiness was (morally) good enough. The sufficiency of a slight contribution to happiness would somewhat depend on what else was available, and a comparative form of satisficing consequentialism would require such alternatives to be taken into account in judging what was good enough. An act producing only slight good might not be judged good enough, even if some non-optimific alternative act producing a great deal of good were regarded as such. (The medic of our example would presumably be wrong to go around simply applying bandages, even if that would slightly ameliorate the situation; but he might still be morally permitted to satisfice in the way mentioned earlier.)

Similarly, where an agent cannot avoid acting in such a way as will lead to the decrease of human happiness, a non-comparative form of satisficing consequentialism, like Bentham's, must presumably treat whatever the agent does as wrong.[17] But it seems more plausible to take into consideration the alternatives to a given act and regard an act as having (circumstantially) good enough consequences if all its alternatives have worse consequences (for the sum of human happiness). So (some of) the difficulties of Bentham's satisficing consequentialist theory of right action are due to its insensitivity to the consequences of alternative actions, and we are thus pointed in the direction of some form of *comparative* satisficing act-consequentialism, in our search for a plausible, interesting, viable alternative to standard optimizing act-consequentialism. (No one has ever suggested a form of non-comparative optimizing act-consequentialism; but such a theory remains a formal possibility and would presumably hold that an act is right only if it produces the (a) best (happiest) situation imaginable. For a being with infinite power the comparative and non-comparative versions of optimizing act-consequentialism tend, of course, to collapse into one another.)

Given, furthermore, our earlier plausible examples of moral satisficing with respect to the relief of suffering, it would seem that satisficing act-consequentialism does best to avoid the radical asymmetry between suffering and happiness entailed by Popper's negative utilitarianism, while at the same time remaining sensitive to the consequences of alternative actions. But having said as much, it is perhaps not necessary at this point to pick and choose among theories that fulfil these desiderata. The important point is that such theories represent a serious alternative to traditional optimizing act-consequentialism and act-utilitarianism, and at this point it would perhaps be a good idea to consider the relative advantages and disadvantages of (plausible versions of) satisficing and optimizing act-consequentialism.

3

Some of the relative strengths of satisficing consequentialism most clearly appear in a certain class of cases, cases where an individual can through his own efforts do a great deal to relieve great human suffering. (I shall play down the distinction between single acts and courses of action in what follows.)

Consider a doctor who wants to help mankind, but is for personal reasons particularly affected by the plight of people in India – perhaps he is attracted to Indian art or religion or very knowledgeable about the history of India. Now an optimizing (utilitarian) act-consequentialist would presumably say that a doctor who volunteered to provide medical assistance to the sick and starving in India should consider whether the suffering there is worse than in other countries (and the opportunities for an outsider to help great enough) so that by going to India he will do or is likely to do more good than he can do elsewhere. And aside from the doctor's motivation and thought processes, it will simply be wrong of him to go to India if some other course of action would do more good for mankind, on any usual optimizing act-consequentialist conception. But many people who wish to relieve human suffering do not consider whether their actions are likely to produce the greatest amount of good possible. When they find a course of action that is likely to make (what they consider) a great (enough) contribution to the relief of suffering and that can compel their personal allegiance and energies, they may act accordingly, without considering whether they might not do more good elsewhere. (Did Schweitzer, before going to Lambaréné, consider whether that was an expectably optimific course of action?) Such moral satisficing does not, from a common-sense moral standpoint, seem wrong; a person who has done a great deal to relieve suffering would not normally be thought to have acted wrongly because she could have done even greater service elsewhere.

Now the reason why, in the present sort of case, less than the best can seem good enough may have something to do with how much good the satisficing individual does and/or aims to do. The good he does is sufficiently great and sufficiently close to the best he could do so as to make it implausible to deny the rightness of his action(s). So for situations of the sort under consideration, it may well be possible formally to elaborate the notion of enoughness as some sort of percentage or other mathematical function of the best results attainable by the agent. I shall not attempt to spell out here the details of any particular plausible way in which this might be attempted. But if satisficing consequentialism has the sort of initial plausibility I think it has, then the way will be open to such a formal elaboration of enoughness and to a consequent precision (over large ranges of cases) about what counts as a morally permissible level of act-consequentialist satisficing.

According to such satisficing act-consequentialism, then, an agent may permissibly choose a course of action that seems to him to do a great deal or a sufficient amount towards the relief of human suffering without considering whether such action is

optimific in the relief of suffering among all the possible courses
of action open to him and without the course of action he chooses
actually being optimific. His sense of what counts as doing a great
deal, or a sufficient amount, towards the relief of suffering may
in part reflect what he knows about the most good that agents
can do in circumstances like his – and what he knows generally
about the world – but in doing the great good he does he need
not seek to do or actually succeed in doing the most good possible.
And, as we have seen, such a view of what an agent may permissibly do comes closer to ordinary moral views about the morality
of benevolence than what is entailed by usual forms of optimizing
act-consequentialism.

One of the chief implausibilities of traditional act-utilitarianism
and act-consequentialism has been their inability to accommodate
moral supererogation. But a satisficing theory that allows less than
the best to be morally permissible can treat it as supererogatory
(and especially praiseworthy) for an agent to do more good than
would be sufficient to ensure the rightness of his actions. Thus, if
the person with special interest in India sacrifices that interest in
order to go somewhere else where (he believes) he can do even
more good, then he does better than (some plausible version of)
satisficing act-consequentialism requires and acts supererogatorily.
But optimizing act-consequentialism will presumably not treat
such action as supererogatory because of its (from a common-
sense standpoint) inordinately strict requirements of beneficence.

Moreover, as we emphasized in previous chapters, critics of
optimizing consequentialism and utilitarianism have recently
tended to focus on one particular way in which such consequentialism implausibly offends against common-sense views of our obligations of beneficence. They have pointed out that (optimizing)
act-consequentialism makes excessive demands on the moral
individual by requiring that she abandon her deepest commitments
and projects whenever these do not serve overall impersonally
judged optimality. We saw in Chapter II that these criticisms are
perhaps best generalized to the claim that act-consequentialism
infringes the individual's *moral autonomy* with respect to the fulfilment of projects and commitments. But what I would like to
suggest here is that at least some of this moral accommodation of
individual desires, commitments and projects can be accomplished
within an entirely (utilitarian) act-consequentialist framework.

Satisficing act-consequentialism of the sort we have been exploring can permit a doctor to work in India, even if he could do more good elsewhere, as long as the amount of good he can do in India is judged to be sufficient. And this then permits the doctor to satisfy his special interest in or concern for things Indian while at the same time fulfilling all that morality can reasonably demand of him. Similarly, a person interested in pure laboratory research might be permitted to pursue such research on condition that it was of such a sort as to be likely to yield great practical benefits for mankind (rather than threaten human survival). Such consequentialism in effect then allows various sorts of *compromise* between the demands of impersonal morality and individual autonomy. To that extent, it allows greater scope for personal preferences and projects than traditional optimizing act-consequentialism does. However, it offers less scope than would be available on most common-sense views of what an agent may permissibly do. For ordinary morality would presumably allow an agent (capable of doing better) to pursue projects that do not contribute very much to overall human well-being, and satisficing consequentialism – unless it maintains a very weak view about what it is to do enough good – will rule such projects out.

However, it is worth noting at this point that none of the moral theories just mentioned offers an all-or-nothing solution to the problem of balancing personal projects and commitments – or more generally, individual autonomy – against impersonal good. Although the point is somewhat obscured by Williams, even optimizing act-consequentialism allows for certain sorts of personal integrity, namely, integrity constituted by the desire precisely to produce the most good possible (help mankind) or by projects which might plausibly be held indirectly to produce the most good that a given agent could achieve. On the other hand, even anti-consequentialists who affirm some sort of common-sense permission to pursue non-optimific projects and commitments typically set limits on what sorts of projects may be thus pursued: the desire to rise in the Mafia is presumably not among them.[18] But within these limits satisficing act-consequentialism occupies an intermediate position; it morally accommodates more kinds of personal preference and personal integrity than traditional optimizing act-consequentialism, but fewer kinds than common-sense anti-consequentialist morality would presumably allow. As such, however,

54

it does offer act-consequentialists the possibility of moving closer to common-sense morality and accommodates a felt need to give greater weight to personal commitments and preferences, while retaining the advantages of a (utilitarian) act-consequentialist framework.[19]

In addition, the choice between satisficing and optimizing consequentialism represents a genuine and difficult problem not only at the level of act evaluation, but also in regard to motives, traits of character, and everything else that can be subjected to consequentialist moral assessment. Is a good (or right) motive, for example, one that has sufficiently good (but not necessarily best) consequences among some set of relevant alternatives or is it one that has the very best consequences among such alternatives? The utilitarian and consequentialist evaluation of motives goes back at least as far as Bentham's *Introduction*, where it is said that motives are good if they produce pleasure or avert pain.[20] Clearly, this represents an embryonic form of *satisficing* motive utilitarianism. And something similar can also be found in Sidgwick's *Methods of Ethics*.[21] On the other hand, R. M. Adams's more recent discussion of motive utilitarianism remains somewhat neutral as between satisficing and optimizing motive utilitarianism in its claim that one motive is *better* than another if *it produces better results*.[22] (Adams later points out some ambiguities in this last phrase, but they are not relevant to our present discussion.) However, Adams too goes on to suggest that a motive may be good or right even if it doesn't have the best possible consequences. And in point of fact satisficing forms of motive-utilitarianism and motive-consequentialism seem generally both more plausible and more interesting than any optimizing version I can think of. Act-consequentialists have had to grant, for example, that on many occasions a father who gives preference to his own children out of love for them may perform a morally wrong action in doing so, but they have attempted to mitigate the harshness and common-sense implausibility of that judgment by adding that the motive of paternal love may nonetheless be a morally good one because it generally leads to good consequences. The father may do what is wrong but he does so out of a morally good motive.[23] However, if a motive had to be in some sense optimific in order to count as morally good, then this irenic ascent (descent?) to the consequential morality of motives might easily fail of its purpose. Is it clear that paternal love generally produces more good than the motive of impartial benevolence, or the love of mankind generally, and are these motives not relevantly alternative to one another? If, on the other hand, we require of good motives only that they generally produce (sufficiently) good results, paternal love need not compete with these other motives in order to count as morally good, so satisficing versions of motive-consequentialism have distinct advantages, for an act-consequentialist and more generally, over optimizing versions of motive-consequentialism.

But if that is so, a question concerning the consistency of moral theories operating at different levels of evaluation immediately arises. In 'Motive Utilitarianism' Adams raises the question whether motive-utilitarianism (motive-consequentialism) is consistent with act-utilitarianism (act-consequentialism) and suggests, subject to certain qualifications, that they are. But in the context of the present discussion and relative to the assumption that one can consistently be both a motive-consequentialist and an act-consequentialist, a further question arises as to whether one can plausibly or consistently be a satisficing consequentialist with regard to some objects of consequentialist evaluation and an optimizing one with respect to others. Can one, for example, reasonably be an optimizing act-utilitarian but a satisficing motive-utilitarian?

To a greater or lesser extent, Bentham, Sidgwick, and Adams all seem to have maintained precisely this combination of views, but their doing so may possibly be due to their having ignored the possibility of satisficing act-utilitarianism rather than to any judgment that optimizing act-utilitarianism fits in well with satisficing motive-utilitarianism. (At the very end of this chapter we shall briefly consider some possible reasons why satisficing consequentialism might easily be ignored or mistakenly ruled out.)

At the very least, the viability and independent plausibility of satisficing motive-consequentialism provide further motivation for satisficing act-consequentialism. They do something to allay fears that there must be something logically or conceptually wrong with any non-optimizing form of act-consequentialism and may even make it easier to regard satisficing versions of act-consequentialism as genuine competitors of the more familiar optimizing variety. Whether there may, in the end, be some sort of inconsistency or tension between optimizing act-consequentialism and satisficing motive-consequentialism (or between satisficing act-consequentialism and optimizing motive-consequentialism) is very difficult to judge, but in terms of sheer symmetry and simplicity, the superior plausibility of satisficing motive-consequentialism seems to recommend a preference for satisficing act-consequentialism as well.

4

We come, finally, to certain views about the nature of morality – views about the fundamental object (or purpose or goal) of morality and about the fundamental or ideal nature of moral motivation – that may be thought to favour, indeed to mandate, optimizing, rather than satisficing, forms of (utilitarian) consequentialism. It has frequently been said, for example, that the object of morality is the general good or universal happiness, and such a view (barring any doubts one may have about morality's having any purpose or object at all) seems to imply that moral schemes – whether act-utilitarian, rule-utilitarian, motive-utilitarian, or any combination of these – must be optimific, e.g., directed toward the greatest happiness of the greatest number. (The problem whether this is best achieved by agent-indirection has no immediate relevance to the issue I am discussing.)

But to assume so would, in fact, be a mistake: it would be to confuse the general, or universal, happiness with the greatest possible general, or universal, happiness, to confuse the well-being of mankind with mankind's greatest possible well-being, and it should be clear – though our discussion of satisficing may help to make it clearer – that these things are not the same. Someone may aim at his *own* happiness in a satisficing way, i.e., without aiming at his own greatest possible happiness; and if someone's *sole aim in life* were to become a good tennis player, it would hardly follow that she aimed at becoming the best player in the world. (Even the latter aim is a satisficing one, since it need not involve aiming to be as good as possible relative to other players, e.g., in a totally different class from everyone else. Some satisficing aims can thus, somewhat misleadingly, be characterized by the use of typical optimizing concepts like bestness.) By the same token it hardly follows from the fact, if it is one, that morality aims at universal well-being or happiness, that it does so in an optimizing way. Yet a failure to distinguish universal happiness or the general well-being from the greatest possible universal happiness or general well-being is characteristic of the entire utilitarian literature, and we find Sidgwick, for example, constantly running these notions together (as well as identifying the desire for one's own happiness alone, egoism, with the desire for one's own greatest happiness).[24]

But from what we have seen, it is possible to aim at the general happiness without aiming at the greatest possible general happiness. And so it is possible to hold a satisficing form of act- (or act-and-motive-) consequentialism consistent with what utilitarians and others have wanted to say about the object of morality. (It is equally possible to maintain a satisficing form of ethical egoism without contradicting or undercutting the most familiar general expressions of that doctrine.) In addition, the most familiar characterizations of (utilitarian) moral motivation also fail to give any preference to optimizing over satisficing forms of consequentialism. For nothing in the idea of impartial, rational benevolence or of universal sympathy entails a desire for the greatest possible human happiness; and even someone with the *highest degree* of impartial rational benevolence or universal sympathy may not always aim for the greatest happiness or well-being possible, since it is possible for many (even all) individuals to be satisficers about their own well-being and it is hardly clear that the greatest possible benevolence or sympathy towards (sympathetic identification with) them would require us to desire their greatest well-being or thus the greatest general well-being of mankind.

It would seem, then, that satisficing consequentialism cannot be excluded on the basis of those general characterizations of the purpose of morality and of moral motivation that have been used to defend (utilitarian) consequentialism generally and optimizing versions of (such) consequentialism in particular. And our whole previous discussion of satisficing individual rationality and of the satisficing elements in the common-sense morality of benevolence should clear the way to making satisficing (act-)consequentialism seem a genuine alternative to prevalent consequentialist views. However, I have here provided only the crudest sketch of how a plausible version of satisficing act-consequentialism might be formulated, and perhaps the ultimate test of the whole notion of (consequentialist) moral satisficing will lie in how appealing more specific and detailed formulations eventually prove to be.

IV

MORALITY AND THE PRACTICAL

The idea of moral satisficing opens up some new possibilities for consequentialism and indicates an area of flexibility within common-sense morality as well. But the fact that we have a genuine and difficult choice to make between optimizing (maximizing) and satisficing versions of consequentialism, the fact that these versions of consequentialism are incompatible moral-theoretic options, may well have some surprising further implications. The conflict between optimizing and satisficing forms of consequentialism ought to provide one focus for the future development of consequentialism, but I hope in the chapters that follow to show that that very conflict may possibly point beyond itself to a kind of consequentialist theory that does not force us to choose between satisficing and optimizing versions. The argument in favour of this possibility – and it is an argument I put forward very tentatively and with many reservations – depends crucially, however, upon certain assumptions about the possibility of non-practical principles concerning right and wrong action. I shall therefore attempt to show in the present chapter how and why both act-consequentialist moral principles and some of the most central principles of our common-sense act-morality are not action-guiding 'imperatives'. Then, in Chapter V, we shall be able to proceed with our defence of the possibility that the conflict between optimizing and satisficing versions of consequentialism may of its own momentum lead to a form of consequentialism where the choice between such theories no longer needs to be made. It will also be argued that the possibility of common-sense moral satisficing together with the existence of non-practical principles in the common-sense morality of right and wrong action may have rather similar and equally 'radical' implications for the development of a theoretically adequate expression of common-sense morality.

1

At present there exists – and for a long time there has existed – a widespread tendency to think of morality – at least the common-sense morality with which we are all most familiar – as some sort of system or code of imperatives, precepts, rules, or principles addressed to moral agents. Thus despite the recent heated debate about the categorical or hypothetical status of moral claims, all parties to the debate seem agreed that (common-sense) moral principles are principles for the guidance of the actions of moral agents: even Philippa Foot, who sparked the recent challenge to Kantian views about the categorical status of morality, treats morality as a system of hypothetical *imperatives*.[1]

The idea that morality consists of a code, system, or whatever for the guiding of action can also be seen in the widespread assumption that moral thinking is a form (one form) of practical thinking, that moral principles are invariably practical. For the idea that morality is (a species of the) practical seems ultimately to derive from Kant, and in Kantian usage 'practical' means something very close to 'for the guidance of agents'.[2] Thus even those who hold that moral principles are merely hypothetical imperatives that do not automatically provide reasons for action, even those who would dispute the Kantian claim that morality is a form of practical *reason*, seem to agree with Kant that morality is fundamentally, invariably practical. In fact, the view that morality is a system of practical principles is both more general and more plausible than the view that morality is a system of imperatives, if the latter is taken entirely literally. But those who speak of morality as a system of hypothetical imperatives also make it clear that their notion of an imperative is not restricted to what is grammatically in the imperative mood (or what can be analysed as being such). Statements that something ought to be done or would be good to do are also to be construed as imperatives and so, presumably, is any normative moral claim that can reasonably be expected to guide moral agents;[3] for such philosophers, then, the thesis that morality is a system of imperatives is roughly equivalent to the Kantian view that morality is a species of the practical.

Now those who share this standpoint naturally wish to allow room for the (non-practical) after-the-fact moral appraisal of actions and agents; but such appraisal is typically seen as derivative from the role of moral principles in guiding action. We may criticize agents (ourselves included) when their behaviour has been out of line with the principles we feel should have been guiding their actions or for acting in *disregard* of such principles, but it is typically held that our picture of moral appraisal should be grounded in a proper understanding of the practical aspects of morality, rather than vice versa. Thus Stuart Hampshire, in a well-known article in *Mind*:

> [T]he issue is – Is the answer to the question 'What are the distinguishing characteristics of sentences expressing moral praise or blame?' necessarily the same as the answer to the question 'What are the distinguishing characteristics of moral problems as they present themselves to us as practical agents?'? Unless these two questions are identical, or unless the first includes the second, much of contemporary moral philosophy is concerned with a relatively trivial side-issue, or is at the very least incomplete. My thesis is that the answer to the second question must contain the answer to the first, but that, if one tries to answer the first question without approaching it as part of the second, the answer will tend to be, not only incomplete, but positively misleading; and that the now most widely accepted philosophical interpretations of moral judgments, their logical status and peculiarities, are radically misleading for this reason. They purport to be logical characterisations of moral judgments and of the distinguishing features of moral arguments, but in these characterisations the *primary* use of moral judgments (= decisions) is largely or even entirely ignored . . . If a purely critical . . . moral judgment . . . is challenged and needs to be defended and justified, it will be justified by the same kind of arguments which one would have used as an agent in practical deliberation.[4]

Though Hampshire doesn't cite anyone who actually denies the moral primacy of the practical, he holds that metaethical views like emotivism and Moorean non-naturalism at the very least obscure that primacy and put an unjustified emphasis upon moral appraisal and criticism. However, within utilitarianism there has been a long tradition of arguing that the principle of utility (or some other consequentialist principle) may constitute the sole valid standard of right and wrong action, even if it is not apt for the regulation of action, for guiding agents in the making of moral decisions.[5] But such views, which reverse the traditional Kantian assumption of the essentially (or primarily) practical character of valid (act-)morality, have been restricted to the consequentialist moral tradition. It has been held to be a distinguishing mark (and sometimes an advantage) of non-consequentialist ordinary morality that it does not allow such a split between the valid standard of morality and the practical moral regulation of actions, that its principles of right and wrong action are action-guiding.[6] And it will be the chief task of the present chapter to show that this supposed difference and advantage are largely illusory. I shall in particular question whether, as in Hampshire's words, 'if a purely critical moral judgment needs to be justified, it will be justified by the same kinds of arguments which one would have used as an agent in practical deliberation.' Important parts of common-sense morality do not answer to this description, and the result will be that even that central part of common-sense morality that concerns right and wrong action cannot properly be described as a system of practical principles or imperatives.

2

Consider what motivates, or often has motivated, the idea that the need for self-defence can justify behaviour that would other-wise be wrong. It is commonly felt that it makes no sense to forbid killing in self-defence (i.e., killing of an aggressor that is necessary in order to preserve one's own life) because of the very depth and strength, in most of us, of the instinct/desire for self-preservation. No proscriptions of killing in self-defence are likely to make the least bit of difference to most people's behaviour, and most of us also feel that killing in self-defence is understandable. We sympathize with the instinct of self-preservation to a sufficient extent that self-protective homicide is not condemned after the fact: not even to the extent of thinking it wrong but excusable through the mitigating circumstance of threat or attack. On the contrary, killing in self-defence is typically considered justified and permissible on the grounds that it is both unrealistic and unfair to expect people not to kill in self-defence. And the depth and strength, indeed the instinctual character, of the desire for self-preservation and/or the impulse to defend oneself against aggression lie behind our belief in the unrealism and unfairness of any contrary expectation. If people didn't value life so much, we would have less sympathy for what was done in defence of life, and the particular character of the impetus towards self-defence makes most of us feel the absurdity and unreasonableness of addressing an injunction forbidding killing in self-defence to ordinary human beings.

Of course, some religious traditions preach a total pacifism that effectively denies the moral legitimacy of killing in self-defence, and injunctions against self-defence presumably can at least partially inhibit the self-defensive behaviour of some individuals. Those who believe in a right to self-defence might attempt to convince pacifists that self-defensive homicide was not wrong, and if they were successful, that would presumably have an effect on the behaviour of some such pacifists in situations where their lives were threatened. So it *makes sense* to address the principle that self-defence is permissible to moral agents, but the sense it makes depends on those agents' having (as most of us might put it) unreasonably severe, almost 'unnatural' moral inhibitions. Most of us are not pacifists and would in the normal course defend ourselves against aggression without, at those very moments, taking account of or being guided by the common-sense moral principle that self-defence is permissible. If acts of self-defence spring from causes as deep and insistent as we are inclined to imagine, then this helps not only to justify self-defence, but also to make it understandable that those acting in self-defence should not be paying heed to or acting from moral injunctions at such moments. And so it would seem that the very factors that make for the common-sense permissibility of killing in self-defence also make it unreasonable to address a principle or precept to that effect to human moral agents in the expectation (or hope) that they will be guided by it when they kill in self-defence. (Wavering pacifists may be guided by it, but we who believe in a right of self-defence find their inhibitions unfortunate and have no desire for other moral agents to resemble them in this respect.)

Consider the contrast with other cases. One may, through promising, incur an obligation to do so something, but later learn that because of unexpected alterations of circumstances, the act one had promised to perform would cause major injury to the promisee. If the promisee is not around to release one from one's promise, one may still feel (correctly, let us assume) that one shouldn't do what one promised, that in the altered circumstances one is permitted (and perhaps even obligated by the 'spirit' of the original promise) not to do what one promised. In this case, surely one's belief that altered circumstances make it permissible not to do what one promised to do is supposed to be a major part of the explanation of why one doesn't do what one promised. And because it seems reasonable to expect people to be influenced by the perception of altered circumstances in this sort of way, a common-sense moral principle asserting that failure to do what one has promised is permissible in certain sorts of altered circumstances can be reasonably addressed to moral agents generally and is thus properly conceived as a *practical* precept of permission. The principle that killing in self-defence is permissible cannot be conceived in this way, however, because some of the very factors that justify it make it (morally) understandable that those who kill in self-defence – even those who do so while knowing that such behaviour is permissible – should not in any large way be *influenced* by the thought that morality allows them to do what they are doing.[7] And in that case the permissibility of killing in self-defence represents a common-sense standard for the moral appraisal of actions, but corresponds to nothing essentially addressable to moral agents and is thus not practical.

Consider, then, what it would be like to address such a standard of permissibility to agents as a practical precept, while holding its rationale to be as we have said. We would in effect be telling people: you are (hereby) permitted to act in self-defence in situations where this very precept will not guide you, and such a form of address is absurd and self-defeating even as exhortation. Alternatively, try to imagine what people would have to be like in order to be convinced that self-protective homicide was permissible and at the same time genuinely influenced by a principle permitting such homicide that *was* properly addressable to them. Such people would presumably have to be able to describe themselves in ways like the following: this large menacing man was coming at me with a meat-cleaver, and because I realized that it was permitted to me in such circumstances to defend myself with violent force, I picked up the gun and . . . Such a description seems eerie and freakish not only because it makes the person acting in self-defence seem so unlike ourselves, but because the cold-bloodedness of the justification it gives threatens to undercut what it is intended to justify. I do not, however, wish absolutely to deny the possibility that killing in self-defence might be justified (in common-sense moral terms) even for someone who lacked a strong desire for self-preservation. Perhaps even a person bent on suicide could justifiably suppose that he had the right to choose his own time to die and a concomitant right of self-defence against serious aggressors. But the justification here seems much less clear-cut, much less forceful, than what we find in ordinary instances of self-protective homicide, and that very fact indicates the importance that considerations of instinctual strength have in our actual rationale for the permissibility of such homicide. The sheer overwhelmingness of our desire to defend ourselves is at least part of the reason why we ordinarily think it not wrong to kill in self-defence and find it morally understandable that someone acting in self-defence should not be guided by moral considerations in so doing.[8]

We shall now see that the considerations that led us to deny the practical character of certain common-sense permissions have similar implications for various common-sense obligations.

3

Those who view ordinary morality as some sort of system of imperatives, or practical rules, typically acknowledge the need to qualify various rules of obligation, and Philippa Foot has claimed in particular that the rule (a rule) stating our obligation to help others should have built into it an exception for cases where the cost to the agent is too great. One has an obligation to help others *except when* the personal cost of doing so would be considerable.[9]

Of course, this last rule is both vague and in need of further qualification, and perhaps the unavoidable cumbersomeness of any fully spelled out rule about helping others tells against this whole way of conceiving morality. But surely, on the other hand, it is entirely natural to think of moral rules and precepts as having exceptions built into them, and my question, in the light of our previous discussion, is whether all appropriately-exceptioned common-sense obligations are encapsulable within precepts, rules, or practical principles.[10]

If self-protective homicide is permissible, then presumably any obligation not to kill must be qualified accordingly and we shall want to say that one has an obligation not to kill (i.e., it is morally wrong to kill) *except in self-defence*. (I ignore other qualifications, for simplicity's sake, in what follows.) But is such a principle of obligation genuinely practical? Presumably, exception-making clauses are genuine parts of a practical principle only if they qualify the practical force of the principle. So if a rule containing exception-making qualifications is properly addressable to moral agents, it must be reasonable and appropriate to expect agents to take those qualifications into account and be influenced by them in action. This is precisely what we do find with many qualified obligations. As we have seen, our putative obligation to do what we have promised is qualified by an exception for cases where, because of altered circumstances, doing what we have promised would cause major injury to the promisee; and it is not unreasonable to expect someone who refrained from doing what he had promised, to do so at least in part because he recognized himself to be in such an exception-making circumstance.

But our supposed obligation not to kill except in self-defence does not function in this way. We cannot reasonably expect someone who kills in self-defence to be substantively influenced, in his actions, by the realization that he is in exceptional circumstances vis-à-vis the obligation not to kill – all for reasons rehearsed at length in the previous section. So if the principle that killing is wrong is genuinely to be qualified by an exception for self-defence, that principle is not properly conceived as a practical principle, as a rule or precept for the guidance of agents, but at most constitutes a valid standard for the moral *appraisal* of human action. The person who kills in self-defence is morally justified in doing what he or she does, even if it is unreasonable to expect

67

that person to take note of, much less be guided by, that fact in the heat of self-protective activity. And the unreasonableness of the expectation is indeed part of the rationale for introducing qualifications about self-defence into the obligation not to kill. Nor is the obligation not to kill the only obligation that needs to be qualified in this sort of way. Our obligation to help others presumably must also contain a qualification for self-defence, and, once again, the rationale for the qualification undercuts the practical character of the obligation. Surely it would be absurd for someone to 'sign-off' from beneficent activities with the thought: 'now I am permitted to stop helping because someone is threatening my life.'

We thus see that various common-sense moral standards of permissibility and obligation cannot be properly conceived as imperatives in any suitably broad sense of the term. And the standards we have mentioned are clearly not outlying facets of our morality, but occupy a central place within it. Nor are exceptions to the practical nature of morality confined to the single, though important case of self-defence. Surely it is in common-sense terms morally permissible for parents to give special preference to their children in situations of grave danger, and obligations to help, to refrain from violence, and indeed not to kill, clearly require qualification to accommodate parental devotion. But given the forceful character of (some) parental devotion, it would be absurd to expect a parent whose child was in danger to be guided by moral considerations in that very situation. In such circumstances, a parent will typically be beyond the reach of moral principles, and a parent who thought to himself 'I am permitted to save my child because family feeling overrides my other obligations' and who acted accordingly would seem to be an unnatural parent. Even if a parent is, from a moral standpoint, justified in rescuing his child from danger, that is not a justification we expect the parent to take into account in so acting. So, once again, we have obligations and permissions (permissibilities) that are not properly regarded as practical. And in the light of these varying examples – and the examples could be multiplied if only space allowed – it should be fairly clear that ordinary morality is not simply a species of the practical, a system of imperatives however broadly construed. And we are also given a new kind of reason to deny the metaethical thesis that moral claims – in particular claims of moral obligation and permission – are all (disguised) prescriptions.[11] Hare's 'descriptivist' critics have powerfully argued that moral and other value claims in general lack the categorical, will-committing force that Hare attributes to them, but have tended to agree with Hare that ordinary moral claims (at least) are always and essentially addressable to moral agents. But if, as we have argued, moral claims are not all practical in this sense, we have yet another reason to deny the universally *prescriptive* force of genuine moral judgments.

4

I think it might be useful at this point to indicate how the views I have just been defending differ from related ideas about morality and about the practical that have appeared in recent philosophical discussions. Philippa Foot, for example, has lately maintained the anti-Kantian thesis that it can sometimes be more virtuous to act from sympathy for someone's plight than out of respect for duty; and Michael Stocker, describing a man who visits a friend in hospital and claims to be doing so from a sense of duty rather than out of fellow-feeling, argues that (the act of) such a person is lacking in moral merit.[12] Such views seem consonant with the idea that there are non-practical aspects of ordinary morality. If someone who visits a sick friend in hospital out of sympathy is (other things equal) more virtuous, more morally meritorious, than the man in Stocker's example, then presumably it is at least sometimes morally better not to be guided by considerations of duty in one's actions.

In that case, we could take an additional step and claim that Stocker's visiting friend would do morally better not even to be influenced by the consideration that it *is* morally better to be guided by sympathy. For if he is thus influenced, he will once again fail to act fully from sympathy and will presumably lack the merit of someone who does. So the greater merit or virtue that Foot and Stocker see in sometimes acting from sympathy is precisely not something that an agent can act upon, though Foot and Stocker do not themselves draw this natural inference from their views and, as I shall now argue, could not easily do so, consistent with other things they say.

To begin with, the idea that certain claims about what is more or less virtuous are not practical is at the very least in tension with Foot's view that (ordinary) morality is a system of hypothetical imperatives, and perhaps the only way one could reasonably avoid inconsistency here would be to claim that questions of greater or less virtue, though not always practical matters, are outside the essential core of morality which is constituted by questions immediately relevant to the rightness and wrongness of actions. If one then maintained that it was not actually *wrong* to visit a hospitalized friend from a sense of duty or virtue, one could perhaps consistently hold that common-sense morality was basically, essentially, a system of practical (hypothetical) imperatives with certain outlying non-practical aspects.

Stocker, however, would face even greater difficulties in acknowledging that some moral matters are non-practical. For elsewhere in his article, he inveighs at length against moral views that cannot be acted on, singling out egoism and act-utilitarianism in this connection; yet he fails to see that his own conclusion about the greater merit of one who acts from sympathy is not a claim that can be acted on. And since (unlike Foot) Stocker explicitly denies that questions of right and wrong are the central questions of morality, he cannot consistently urge the insignificance of the non-practical moral conclusion we have distilled from his example and his assumptions about it.

In the light of these difficulties, it is perhaps not clear whether questions of greater or less merit or virtue *are* central to ordinary morality. But in that case, the significance of our earlier examples becomes especially vivid. For these concerned issues that everyone recognizes to be of fundamental moral importance, and their non-practical character can *leave no doubt* that common-sense morality is not a system of imperatives. There are also, moreover, reasons to doubt whether Foot and Stocker are right to ascribe (other things being equal) greater moral merit, or virtue, to someone who visits a sick friend out of sympathy rather than from a sense of duty. The man who acts from duty is not the kind of friend most of us would want; perhaps he is no friend at all, given his cold-blooded approach to friendship. And certainly we are likely to think less well of him than of someone who acts from sympathy. But even those, like Hume, who have emphasized the sympathetic underpinnings of morality have also stressed the need for moral dispositions that can outlast flagging sympathies and overcome outright antagonisms, and surely the man who acts from duty may evince steadier tendencies to do the right thing than someone whose visit was primarily motivated by sympathy. So perhaps our lower regard for the visitor who acts self-consciously from duty is a matter of finding the man less attractive as a human being than the friends we hope to have, rather than of finding him *morally* defective. It is thus not at all clear that Stocker's man really is less virtuous or morally meritorious than the simpatico person who acts from sympathy. And that is yet another reason to stress our earlier examples in any attempt to show that common-sense morality is not a species of the practical. For there is much more agreement about the permissibility of killing in self-defence (and even of favouring one's children) than about the greater *moral* merit of someone whose good deeds are done from sympathy.

Of course, it may seem plausible and uncontroversial in common-sense terms to assert an obligation to visit sick friends in hospital, but there is nothing non-practical about this obligation, if it exists. Human sympathies can flag, and if we believe that people ought to visit sick friends, then we shall want someone whose friendly feeling does flag at least to be guided by (this very) moral precept. Thus the circumstances that might make us invoke a moral principle concerning the *duties* of friendship are precisely those in which we would need that principle to play a practical role. The earlier-discussed principles regarding self-defence seem much less practical, by comparison, because the kind of case that induces us to qualify the obligation not to kill is (as we have seen) typically one in which people are understandably beyond the 'reach' of moral principles. So the circumstances that most clearly call for a qualification in the general obligation not to kill are circumstances in which the qualification *lacks* a practical moral function; and that is why I believe that the examples of self-defence (and to a lesser extent of parental favouritism) provide the best means of establishing the non-practical character of some of our most basic common-sense moral obligations and permissions.[13]

On the other hand, if one is sufficiently wedded to the assumption that principles of right and wrong must be practical, one might at this point be led to deny what we have been saying and maintain, instead, that self-defence (or family favouritism) is altogether outside the scope of (common-sense) morality, neither morally justified (permissible, all right) nor morally unjustified (impermissible, wrong). And something like this line has in fact been taken, at least with regard to supposed permissions to favour one's own family, by Bernard Williams in 'Persons, Character and Morality'.[14] But the conclusion that self-defence and family favouritism are outside morality would force us to renounce some very plausible and deep-seated moral ideas: e.g., the belief that there is such a thing as justifiable homicide (and a *right* of self-defence) and the idea that the moral obligation not to kill needs to be *qualified* for cases of self-defence. It makes more sense to reject the original assumption, that principles of right and wrong must be practical, which leads to such results.

As I mentioned earlier, suggestions of a divergence between practical moral thinking and moral appraisal are also to be found within the utilitarian tradition. Act-utilitarians frequently advance utilitarian arguments for holding that not everyone should attempt to follow the principle of utility and that it can be wrong to inculcate act-utilitarianism in others. And even in those favourable circumstances where a utilitarian finds it useful and right to address the principle of utility to moral agents, he may also be hoping that those agents will sometimes *not* be motivated by it. For utilitarians often maintain that one can upon occasion achieve more good by acting spontaneously (e.g., from love or friendship) than by trying to maximize utility.[15] For all these reasons, then, the act-utilitarian principle that one has an obligation to do what maximizes utility may embody a standard of act-appraisal that is at best imperfectly apt for the guidance of moral agents.[16]

Both Bernard Williams and Michael Stocker have taken act-utilitarianism to task for allowing even a partial divergence between appraisal and the practical regulation of action,[17] but we should be suspicious of this sort of criticism because our earlier discussion makes it abundantly clear that non-utilitarians must also acknowledge a split between the critical and the practical. The examples of self-defence and parental devotion yield common-sense principles of act-appraisal that cannot reasonably be expected to govern action, and so our common-sense act-morality cannot be held superior to act-consequentialism in virtue of the invariably (essentially) practical character of its standards of right and wrong action.[18]

On the other hand, the fact that even a utilitarian can acknowledge the value of spontaneity in action can help us to see that the divorce between practical precepts and standards of act-appraisal also exists outside of morality (narrowly conceived). No one doubts that it is good (or best) to be spontaneous on occasion, and yet, as has often been noted, someone who acts spontaneously cannot be acting out of a regard for the benefits of so acting.[19] Some good things are spoiled if we think about them, and their value, too much, and it seems clear enough that the value of (occasional) spontaneity cannot be properly embodied within any practical principle, moral or otherwise. So there are areas outside of morality proper where standards of act-evaluation and act-appraisal are simply not practical, and this point, in its application to questions of human welfare, may well have been appreciated for some time now. It has perhaps been less well appreciated, however, that similar considerations apply to the moral. Morality, even common-sense morality, cannot be distinguished from other forms of evaluation by its universally practical character, but, like the ethics of human welfare, embodies some standards for the critical appraisal of actions that cannot sensibly be translated into precepts addressed to agents.

We found this to be true of common-sense morality in particular largely because of the way various powerful human feelings and reactions seem to carve out a space of moral immunity that correspondingly restricts the scope of our moral obligations. Interestingly enough, however, facts about human feeling and reaction do not similarly induce us to qualify the precepts of etiquette. It is bad manners to eat peas with a knife, but no one is in the least inclined to qualify that claim into: it is bad manners to eat peas with a knife except in self-defence. Nor is it a principle of etiquette that one should not eat peas with a knife except in order to save one's own children. This difference between etiquette and morality may be of some importance and clearly calls for explanation; but for our present purposes, it chiefly serves to suggest the purely practical character of etiquette. The considerations that forced us earlier to acknowledge that morality is not a species of the practical do not seem to apply to good manners, and correct etiquette may thus well constitute a system of (hypothetical) imperatives of the kind that ordinary morality is widely thought to be.

If, for the reasons given above, it is a mistake to think of morality as universally practical, then we must also reject Hampshire's claim that a proper understanding of moral problems as they present themselves to ordinary moral agents can generate a proper understanding of moral criticism. For as we have seen, some standards of moral criticism are based precisely on its being understandable that certain sorts of considerations should *not* occur to or influence moral agents. Are we to conclude, then, that in morality the critical standpoint is prior to that of the agent? Not necessarily. We would presumably not want to base such a claim on the outmoded metaethical theories that (Hampshire believes) earlier supported such a position. And there may well be aspects of moral agency that cannot properly be understood in moral-critical terms, so that neither the agential nor the critical standpoint will have clear priority. But I have, for the moment, no idea what those aspects might be, and I would like to suggest one way in which the point of view of ordinary moral agents might turn out to be derivative from that of common-sense moral appraisal.

It may be possible to think of common-sense moral criticism as containing principles with both practical and non-practical qualifications, e.g., the principle: it is wrong to kill except in self-defence or in one's capacity as an official state executioner, etc. (It is not terribly important that this illustrative principle be plausible.) Because such a principle contains a non-practical qualification, it cannot itself be thought of as practical. But since moral criticism justifies such qualifications in terms of their understandable non-occurrence to agents, it presumably also has the means to tell us which qualifications in its principles are non-practical and thus, more significantly, which qualifications in its principles need to be deleted in order to arrive at principles that *can* properly be construed as practical. Now if all the practical principles of common-sense morality could be generated from its critical standards in this way – and we have at this point been given no reason to believe the contrary – then critical common-sense morality would have the resources to generate and justify the principles of ordinary action-guiding morality, and the latter would in at least one clear sense be derivative from the former.

It should be added, however, that even non-practical common-sense (moral) principles of the sort we have been discussing may have various practical *implications*. For example, the principle that it is good to be spontaneous may influence (non-spontaneous) decisions about how to educate children; and the principle that self-defensive homicide is permissible (not wrong) may persuade someone to buy a gun for his home or convince a jury to return a verdict of 'not guilty'. But in cases such as these, the non-practical principle involved is only useful in deciding whether to do something *not mentioned* by the principle itself. It thus has what we might call indirect practical uses, without thereby counting as practical. For on our usual understanding of the notion, practical principles (precepts, imperatives) guide an agent towards the doing of things that they themselves mention and recommend.

Finally, nothing we have said above should be taken as implying that we are not, outside of philosophy, chiefly interested in correct moral appraisal for the guidance it gives us as moral agents. Nor does anything we have said entail a moral intellectualism according to which the moral life is primarily a matter of making the right critical judgments, deriving the right practical precepts from them, and then acting according to the latter. Quite to the contrary, one of the main points here has been that people may be morally justified when they act from certain impulses and feelings without paying any attention to moral principles or justifications. We have seen that, far from simply governing human life, ordinary morality is itself shaped, limited, influenced, even governed by factors outside itself, and self-aware practical moral thought – whether of a consequentialist or common-sense variety – floats upon a deeper, fuller life that occasionally drives out all thought about morality. Indeed, there is a definite sense in which our present standpoint stresses the practical aspects of (ordinary) morality far more than does the widely influential Kantian tradition that holds that all aspects of the moral are reflected in the reasoning of moral agents and that morally right action should be governed by the thought of certain moral precepts. For if we understand the practical not (in the philosophically usual, Kantian sense) as entailing a regard for action-guiding principles, but rather in that everyday sense in which it contrasts with everything intellectual and intellectualistic, then surely the argument of the present chapter makes (ordinary) morality as a whole seem much *more* practical than it is usually taken to be.

75

V

SCALAR MORALITY

In Chapter III I argued that various forms of satisficing consequentialism are genuine alternatives to their optimizing consequentialist counterparts. But in the present chapter I would like to show that the discussion of Chapter IV and an acknowledgment of the distinction between satisficing and optimizing consequentialism may actually carry us beyond this distinction to a point where we no longer feel the need to *choose between* these two forms of consequentialism. In other words, once we grant that (valid) principles of right and wrong action need not be practical and it is seen that nothing in the nature of moral terms, moral motivation or the aims of morality forces us to opt for an optimizing rather than a satisficing form of consequentialism or utilitarianism, further reasons may persuade the consequentialist to remain neutral between these alternatives. And our task in the present chapter will be to understand *how* a properly consequentialist moral theory could remain neutral between these alternatives and to see what advantage such a neutral theory might have over satisficing and optimizing moral conceptions. The sort of neutral theory I have in mind I shall call, for reasons to be made clear in what follows, scalar consequentialism, and after considering some of the advantages of this sort of theory, both in act and motive versions, I shall go on to examine the possibility that the common-sense morality of benevolence (beneficence) may also best be understood in scalar – rather than more traditional – terms.

Chapter III already contains some hints about what one form of scalar consequentialism might be like. We there pointed out that the particular form of motive-utilitarianism Robert Adams (following Sidgwick)[1] proposes seems (at least in one of his formulations) neutral between satisficing and optimizing versions of such utilitarianism. Adams merely states that one motive is better than another if it has better consequences than that other, and this says nothing about when something counts as a *good* motive. It leaves open the possibility that only a motive with the best sort of consequences (relative to relevant alternatives) can be accounted good, but also allows for the possibility that a motive with good enough consequences less than the best might qualify as good. Now, as I mentioned earlier, most motive-consequentialists seem in fact to have held a satisficing version of that doctrine, but the neutral version Adams mentions does not actually commit one to either a satisficing or optimizing form of (utilitarian) motive-consequentialism, and what I would like to explore at this point is the possibility of there being reasons for maintaining the neutral version *in preference to* either the optimizing or the satisficing version. Some of the difficulties of deciding *between* satisficing and optimizing motive-consequentialism may give us reason to believe that neither of them can represent an entirely satisfactory form of motive-consequentialism and that the most adequate kind of motive-consequentialism is a *scalar theory* that makes only comparative judgments of better or worse between motives.

To begin with, how important really is it to decide between satisficing and optimizing motive-consequentialism? The optimizing motive-consequentialist holds that only a motive with optimal consequences counts as a good motive. But as a good consequentialist has he any reason to be thus restrictive about the goodness of motives? (Would he similarly wish to restrict bad motives to those with 'pessimal' consequences?) On the other hand, there also seems to be no reason why the satisficing motive-consequentialist should insist that a motive with less than optimal consequences can qualify as a good one.[2] And, even granting that less than the best can be good enough, it is hard to see how a satisficing consequentialist could justify one level of good results rather than another as being the proper or natural (rough) dividing line between good and non-good (though not necessarily bad) motives.

What seems to be the case, rather, is that the (presumably valid) scale of objectively better and worse consequences (of a motive) carries with it no natural or non-arbitrary resting place for a distinction between good and bad motives, and this seems to imply that any attempt to draw such a distinction (even in a way that allows for vagueness) will reflect some sort of (possibly useful) convention, not an objectively significant fact. Let me suggest a parallel.

It seems plausible to hold, for example, that baldness (bald-headedness) is, objectively speaking, a matter of degree, a comparative matter except at the limits. Although, in other words, a person with all his (normal complement of head) hair clearly (determinately) isn't bald and someone with absolutely no hair on his head clearly (determinately) is, there is no actual dividing line in between that enables one to make an objectively significant distinction between people who are and people who are not bald. Indeed, different societies (languages) might conventionally put the (vagueness-permitting) dividing line between bald and not bald in different places, but, given agreement on what counts as more and less bald, no one of those societies would have a superior understanding of the objective phenomenon of baldness. But by the same token, there is no reason to think a society that refused to draw such a line and restricted itself to comparative judgments (except at the limits) would be at a baldness-theoretic disadvantage compared with these other societies, would understand any less about the objective phenomenon of (the objective facts about) baldness. And that seems to suggest that drawing a dividing line between baldness and non-baldness may not *add* anything to one's knowledge about baldness, if one has a sufficient understanding of comparative baldness, of baldness as a scalar phenomenon.

But then, by the same token, it might be said that a purely scalar motive-consequentialism would embody as complete and objective a (consequentialist) understanding of the morality of motives as any optimizing or satisficing theory that drew a line between good and non-good motives. There seems to be no reason to think, or at least for a consequentialist to think, that any such dividing line can be any more non-conventional or objectively justified than a similar line between baldness and non-baldness.

Of course, as with baldness, a scalar theory of the morality of motives might allow itself to make non-comparative judgments at the limits and claim that a motive with no good consequences (on balance, overall) was determinately not good and one with optimal consequences (among relevant alternatives) determinately good. But it would make no other non-comparative judgments. And such a theory would not only capture all the objective moral facts (phenomena) described by a satisficing or optimizing form of motive-consequentialism, but would seem to have a certain advantage over such theories by virtue of its refusal (except minimally and non-controversially) to distinguish good from non-good motives. For if (as typically) the motive-consequentialist (motive-utilitarian) is seeking, like other consequentialists, to present an objective moral view of things, an adequate (if limited) moral theory – and nothing more – then the inclusion of an objectively unjustified distinction regarding good motives threatens his goal of presenting an objective moral theory. Thus a consequentialist morality of motives can as a whole embody an objective moral viewpoint, only if it avoids arbitrary dividing lines. And given such fundamental moral-theoretic goals, there is a reason to prefer a scalar motive-consequentialism over any satisficing or optimizing form of motive-consequentialism – even one that, in addition to drawing dividing lines, also depicts all the relevant scalar phenomena. So I believe we have reason to prefer a scalar form of motive-consequentialism over any optimizing or satisficing version, although a consequentialist might justifiably wish, for reasons of metaethical completeness, to append to his scalar motive-consequentialism his reasons for not going beyond such a theory and providing a dividing line between good and non-good motives. For presumably it is a completely objective, non-arbitrary, non-conventional fact (if it is a fact at all) that such dividing lines are themselves arbitrary and conventional.

What has just been said about goodness in motives can presumably for similar reasons be said about the goodness of consciences, characters (total constellations of character traits), and even perhaps persons. A consequentialist moral theory of goodness of character, for example, might justifiably prefer to rank total character-constellations as better or worse according to their consequences without saying anything about what counted, absolutely, as (a) good character. But consequentialism (or utilitarianism) has primarily and most typically taken the form of a moral theory about actions, and I would like now to consider whether a consequentialist satisfied with a scalar morality of motives should not also be contented with a purely scalar morality of actions.

Act-consequentialists have almost always assumed that an act is right (or morally good) if and only if it has consequences at least as good as any of its alternatives. But this is an optimizing act-morality, and we have previously seen the possibility of a form of act-consequentialism that made room for moral satisficing and treated an act as right if its consequences were good enough (even though less than the best). However, in the light of what has been said about baldness and the goodness of motives, we may well ask whether there can be any objective grounds for choosing between optimizing and satisficing forms of act-consequentialism (or act-utilitarianism). Once we see satisficing act-consequentialism as a genuine alternative to the traditional optimizing kind, once we see that there *is* an act-consequentialist alternative to optimizing conceptions of the morality of actions, it becomes clear that the latter draw a line between right and wrong actions that is far from inevitable. One may hold that an act is right only if its consequences are optimal, but the possibility of a less stringent consequentialist standard of right action can make the consequentialist wonder whether, as in the case of baldness, any such dividing line between right and wrong action can be other than conventional. The choice between satisficing and optimizing act-consequentialism would then be seen as involving a somewhat arbitrary decision about when the consequences of acts were good enough to qualify them as morally right, but by the same token any choice between differently stringent forms of satisficing act-consequentialism would also have to be seen as arbitrary. No dividing line between right and wrong action would be thought of as corresponding to anything objectively valid, and the desire to present a non-arbitrary consequentialist theory of the morality of actions would presumably then lead one to espouse a scalar form of act-consequentialism according to which an act *a* counts as morally better than an alternative *b* just in case *a* has better consequences than *b*.[3] As far as I know, no one has ever offered a purely scalar version of act-consequentialism of the sort Adams, briefly and tentatively, offers as an example of motive-consequentialism. But I believe that the motivation for scalar consequentialism is rather similar at the level of acts to what can be made out at the level of motives.

However, in order to defend such a view, we must consider one important objection to such a similar treatment of acts and motives, the objection, namely, that while a morality of motives need not, indeed cannot, be practical, a morality of actions must essentially be so.

This objection becomes relevant to the issue of scalar act-consequentialism through the consideration that such a morality, through failing to provide a dividing line between right and wrong actions, may fail to provide the kind of guidance for agents that any objectively valid morality might be thought essentially to provide. But such a criticism of scalar act-consequentialism can have very little force, I think, for most act-consequentialists. Many act-utilitarians, for example, have been committed to the idea that the principle of utility both constitutes the sole objective standard of right action, yet cannot or should not always, or even usually, function as a practical guide for human beings. As I mentioned in the previous chapter, some utilitarians have held that for some agents in some circumstances it may be too difficult to make use of the principle of utility; and that in a large number of cases – perhaps even in general – one may do more good by not following the principle (and, possibly, following some other moral principle) than by following it.

Now, presumably, if one is a (utilitarian) act-consequentialist, one will believe that there is a need for some sort of moral principles to govern conduct, but to the extent one holds that the non-practical principle of utility or any other non-practical consequentialist principle constitutes the sole objective standard of right action, one will have to view these other principles merely as useful practical expedients or rules of thumb. And this way of distinguishing between (e.g.) the principle of utility as a valid moral standard and merely useful practical moral principles opens the way to a similar defence of scalar act-consequentialism or act-utilitarianism. For if the objective moral standard needn't share the practical character of the moral rules or principles that are needed to guide everyday action, there will, presumably, also be no need for that standard to draw the sort of distinction between right and wrong action that enables the ordinary rules to be so practically effective. And in that case some form of scalar act-consequentialism may represent the sole objective truth about the morality of actions while some other set of non-scalar and presumably non-consequentialist rules or principles provided people with the sort of useful practical guidance which any consequentialist would herself wish, on consequentialist grounds, to see people provided with. If the practical need for non-consequentialist principles is fully compatible with the sole validity of act-consequentialism as a moral standard, so too, then, may the practical need for non-scalar principles offer no threat to our earlier claim that a scalar form of act-consequentialism has the best chance of providing a non-arbitrary and objectively valid act-consequentialist standard (theory) of morality.

2

What implications, then, does the possibility of scalar forms of consequentialism have for the way we regard non-consequentialist common-sense morality? It has already been pointed out that the intuitive morality of common-sense contains a part – roughly corresponding to the morality of benevolence – where the consideration of good consequences plays an especially important role. If any area of common-sense moral thinking is likely to be affected by what has just been said in favour of scalar consequentialism, I think it is our thoughts and attitudes regarding duties to benefit others. And what may particularly favour a scalar interpretation or revision of the common-sense morality of benevolence are certain difficulties that seem to arise from the common-sense standpoint itself in connection with duties to help people less fortunate than ourselves.

The fact of widespread human suffering makes a moral claim on us not only from the utilitarian or consequentialist point of view, but on common-sense moral grounds as well. Even apart from any responsibility we may have for having made less fortunate other people less well off than they could have been,[4] the common-sense morality of benevolent action seems to regard it as in general wrong never to do anything for those less fortunate people whom one is in a position to help and as morally better to do more for such people rather than less, to sacrifice more of one's own well-being rather than less in order to give aid to the less fortunate.

But this, of course, doesn't tell us how much one must give in order to give what one morally ought to give, to fulfil one's (imperfect) duty of benevolence. It assumes that it is wrong never to give aid to those worse off than oneself (when one can easily do so, etc.).[5] And it also assumes that it is morally acceptable and morally best (when this involves no violation of side-constraints, etc.) to give all one has to the less fortunate, or, at least, to reduce oneself to the (presumably rising) level of well-being of those one should be trying to help. But these assumptions say nothing about the wide spectrum of cases between giving nothing and giving, as it were, one's all; and controversy, disagreement, and indecision over where, in that spectrum, the (rough) dividing line between duties and supererogations of benevolence should be drawn have featured time and time again in ethical discussions.

One idea, for example, that has frequently been found appealing both by writers on ethics and by non-philosophers has been the principle of tithing, of giving a tenth of all one has earned or has to those (if any) who have less than oneself. Understood as a duty and not a supererogatory ideal, such a principle would require some sacrifice beyond what a merely occasional donation to charity would entail: the person with a comfortable income might have to do without a video tape-recorder or a second car, but compliance with the principle would hardly need to affect an individual's basic life style or most fundamental life plans. Given various plausible assumptions, therefore, a principle of tithing would come quite close to requiring what would be required of individuals under a less quantitative principle which claimed that one has an obligation to act in order to relieve or prevent human suffering to the (full) extent that doing so does not interfere with one's basic life plans, life style, or way of life. Such a principle would claim, in effect, that one must give as much as one can give without affecting one's basic life plans to those less fortunate than oneself;[6] and it is clearly much more demanding than the mere requirement, as some philosophers and certainly many others would have it, that one occasionally (or even frequently) give to charity.

But such conceptions of moral duty in fact seem relatively undemanding when ranged against certain other views that have been advocated about our duties to others, and these other views, I think, also have some appeal at the level of ordinary moral intuitions. The sort of view I had in mind here is not any traditional variety of utilitarianism or consequentialism; for it is somewhat unclear – at least it is somewhat unclear to me – just what sort of appeal traditional utilitarianism is capable of making to ordinary moral intuitions. But in recent years Peter Singer has advocated ideas about our moral obligations to others which, though less demanding, say, than the principle of utility, are also considerably more demanding than the sorts of views mentioned above. Yet I believe Singer's conception of our moral obligations is capable of exerting a considerable appeal at the level of common-sense morality.

According to Singer, if it is in our power to prevent something bad from happening without sacrificing anything of comparable moral importance, we ought, morally, to do it.[7] And most ordinary people would, indeed, find such a principle plausible upon first hearing it. Yet the principle, as Singer himself shows, has radical implications that those who find it initially appealing usually do not suspect. For if one assumes, as most of us would be inclined to do, that whether I succeed in maintaining my life style or life projects is (in almost all cases) not as morally important as whether someone dies of (or suffers from) disease or starvation, then it seems to follow that those of us with comfortable incomes ought to spend most of that income – not a tenth, but more like nine-tenths – for the relief of famine and disease in the Third World or elsewhere. (I assume here that our money can effectively be used towards these ends.) Alternatively, we may have to give up our present source(s) of income, in order to go off and devote ourselves to the relief of suffering in the Third World or elsewhere.

Thus Singer's initially appealing principle in the end implies a very demanding view of individual moral obligations, and because that implied view runs counter to ordinary moral beliefs, those who come to recognize the implications of Singer's original principle frequently come to have doubts about it, to find it less appealing, and consequently perhaps to find themselves unable to decide between a (covertly) demanding principle of benevolence like Singer's and the sorts of less-demanding principles mentioned above. The disagreement or divergence between more and less demanding conceptions of our duties of benevolence is, in fact, quite difficult to resolve in any satisfactory way. The fact is, I think, that all these moral conceptions have some sort of common-sense appeal, and I therefore wonder whether common-sense morality has within itself the resources for settling the issue among these rival views. That very fact, however, can make one wonder, in turn, whether common-sense moral intuitions are best served by the assumption that one of these views must be the correct one, however difficult it may be to determine which. For all these views draw a (rough) dividing line between morally necessary and morally supererogatory or optional benevolence, and the difficulty of getting any sort of convincing permanent agreement about which of them draws the line in the right place may therefore indicate that the lines they respectively draw between necessary and optional benevolence are all *arbitrary* from a common-sense moral standpoint (i.e., with respect to the best-organized totality of our common-sense intuitions and beliefs).

In that case the analogy with baldness and with what we have said about satisficing and optimizing consequentialism becomes apparent, and we are given reason to take seriously the possibility that our common-sense morality of benevolence is best understood, or most objectively expressed, in scalar form. Perhaps, in other words, we should on common-sense grounds limit our conception of the morality of benevolent action to those uncontroversial claims about what is morally better and worse that are common to all the above non-scalar claims about our obligations of benevolence, together, perhaps, with those relatively uncontroversial positive judgments about what is right and wrong that we also mentioned above. Both relatively demanding and relatively undemanding views of benevolence would agree, presumably, that it is (other things being equal) morally better to give or sacrifice more rather than less for the benefit of less fortunate others; and all such theories seem to agree about the wrongness of being unwilling ever to give charitably or to help those who are suffering or in distress (through no fault of one's own) and about the moral acceptability of giving one's all for the relief of others. The disagreements are all about the positive evaluation in terms of right and wrong of cases that lie somewhere in between these extremes, and to the extent it seems plausible to invoke the analogy with baldness, we may have good reason to expunge all such positive judgments from an ideally objective common-sense-based morality of benevolent action[8] and frame such a morality in scalar terms.

3

If there is any objection to be made to the idea of a scalar version of the common-sense morality of benevolence, it must, I think, come from a suspicion that scalar morality is not sufficiently action-guiding. Consequentialists, of course, have been willing to grant that the sole valid principle of (act-)morality might not be practically useful, and they have often sought, therefore, to complement their objective standard of right action with some view about the way other, non-consequentialist principles might usefully regulate human action. But defenders of common-sense morality have often taken it to be an advantage of the view they defend that it requires no such split between valid morality and the practical regulation of action,[9] and they have tended to hold that any valid morality governing actions (as opposed to one governing motives or other traits not under the fairly immediate control of the will) must by its very nature provide practical advice. Since a scalar morality of benevolent actions tells us only what actions are better than others, not what actions are right and wrong, or thus, it would seem, what actions to *do*, it is natural, on a view such as the above, to conclude that a scalar morality of benevolence cannot express the full moral truth about benevolence. Something important would, from the standpoint of ordinary morality, be missing. (This line of reasoning would presumably go on to say that there must be some non-arbitrary, though perhaps hard to find, way to distinguish between duties and supererogations of benevolence because such a distinction is essential to an objective, fully practical morality of actions.)

There are, however, a number of ways in which the above argument can be questioned. The contrast drawn in the name of common-sense morality between the action-guiding principles of such morality and defectively practical act-consequentialist principles is not, as we saw in the last chapter, so stark as it initially seems. The ordinary morality of right and wrong action contains non-practical principles concerning killing and benevolence in relation both to self-defence and to family concerns, and one highly relevant example of these would be the qualification, in some appropriate principle of benevolence, that permitted one not to rescue some person in distress when one was oneself put under threat of death by an attacker. So even the non-scalar common-sense morality of benevolent action contains non-practical principles, and it would be difficult indeed, in the name of common-sense, to deny the validity of such principles. The permissibility of self-defence is as commonsensical and intuitive as anything in the ordinary morality of right and wrong action, so it would appear that the defender of such morality cannot invoke the invariably practical character of its principles in order to cast doubt on the idea of a wholly scalar morality of benevolence.

Of course, the defender of common-sense morality might then rejoin that although certain central principles of ordinary morality are not action-guiding, not imperatives, still ordinary morality as a whole, and important parts of it, like the morality of benevolence, lose their point if one seeks to detach them from any action-guiding function. But this particular point can in fact be granted by a proponent of a scalar common-sense morality of benevolence. After all, even judgments of morally better and worse can guide a moral agent in one direction or another, so if the opponent of scalar benevolence has any relevant criticism to make here, it must, I think, involve the stronger claim that (any large part of) ordinary morality must *tell us what to do*. For this is something which it is tempting to suppose claims of better and worse cannot do, but claims of right and wrong always do.

But to what extent do claims that one or another possible action is right or wrong invariably tell the moral agent what to do? In the recent anti-consequentialist literature, it has been argued, for example, that moral tragedy is possible, that one may through no fault of one's own get into a situation where one will act wrongly whatever one does (as an agent – if one goes crazy trying to decide what to do, one may not act wrongly but the going crazy is not an action and one then loses one's status as an agent). And in such cases the judgment that an action is wrong precisely cannot tell one what to do.[10]

In addition, and more commonly, one may be in a situation where more than one possible action is morally acceptable and again no judgment of right or wrong or better or worse can tell one which one of those actions to perform. (Even the fact that one of those actions is better than all the others may not tell one what to do, since common-sense often allows one permissibly to fail to do what is morally best and one may as a moral agent not be *interested* in doing what is best.) So judgments of right and wrong concerning particular actions need not be action-guiding in the strong sense of telling one what to do, of fully resolving practical perplexity. It is thus not clear how we can say that any major area of common-sense morality must be capable of telling us what to do in situations where its principles apply, or, therefore, how a scalar common-sense morality of benevolence can be faulted for not telling us what to do.

I think, moreover, that some of the objection to a scalar morality of benevolence comes from underestimating the extent to which such a morality could function in an action-guiding way. Some moral individuals may be concerned simply with 'getting by' morally, with doing no more than they feel morality actually demands of them. For them, the fact that an action is wrong has practical force in a way that judgments of better and worse, right and best, may not. Still other people are amoral enough so that even judgments of wrongness are insufficient to tell them what not to do. But someone with strong moral motivation may be guided by all these judgments. The claim that one action is better than another may tend to make him reject the latter, and the claim that one action is better than all its alternatives may often motivate him to do that very action. For such a person, judgments of better and worse may be strongly action-guiding, even if they might not be for someone who wished merely to get by with no wrongdoing. So whether someone who thought in purely scalar moral terms would be guided by the judgments of such a morality would depend, in part, on how motivated he was to do what was better rather than worse. But this feature hardly distinguishes scalar morality from non-scalar common-sensism, since the action-guiding power of a morality making both comparative and positive judgments will likewise depend both on how inclined people are to do better rather than worse actions *and on how inclined they are to do what is right*. In fact, a scalar morality of benevolent actions might even be 'moralific', i.e., lead people to do better actions than they would do if they attempted to follow a non-scalar morality. Just as people who tried to live up to some highly demanding non-scalar morality of benevolence might become demoralized by their failures to do as they ought and so end by doing morally worse things than people who tried to follow some less demanding non-scalar morality, so too might a scalar morality produce morally better actions in its adherents than any morality that distinguished between right and wrong.[11] People may well end up acting better when faced with comparative moral judgments than with potentially guilt-and-anxiety provoking judgments of right and wrong. In the light of all the above it is hardly clear that a scalar morality of benevolence cannot constitute the most objective and adequate expression of our common-sense views in this area.

Of course, if a scalar view provides the most adequate expression of our common-sense morality of benevolence, then this area of common-sense morality may not offer the sort of practical guidance we initially expected from it. Perplexed by the question how much to give to others less fortunate than ourselves and, in particular, moved by the plight of people in the Third World to wonder whether we must abandon our comfortable lives in order to help them, we often look to moral philosophy for guidance, and a number of specific non-scalar views have been developed and advocated in response to our perplexities. Unfortunately, the views that have been developed conflict and threaten to continue conflicting without assuming any one direction towards final resolution, and in that state of things, our present state, we may well wonder whether the sort of, the amount of, practical guidance that we sought in this area is in principle really available. In this respect our situation with regard to benevolence may be like that which common-sense deontological restrictions ultimately place us in. For those restrictions are often invoked in order to steel the individual against taking some option tempting in terms of its general good consequences,[12] and are thought, therefore, to settle the matter of what to do in situations where that question seems (or might otherwise seem) difficult to answer. But in recent years, it has been argued that deontological restrictions on consequentialist thinking bring in their wake the possibility of morally tragic cases where deontological morality at least is incapable of prescribing what to do and thus of providing the sort of guidance one hoped, or might have hoped, it would give.

Our situation in regard to the common-sense morality of benevolence may be relevantly similar to this: we may here have one more area where common-sense morality, in seeking completeness and objectivity, disappoints our desire for clearcut moral guidance. And if there is no less, then I also think there is no more reason to reject scalar moral benevolence on this account than to reject those deontological restrictions that threaten our freedom from undeserved moral tragedy. If in the latter case a proper working out of our moral sense of things *provides too much*: namely, contradictory yet indefeasible duties that make it impossible to avoid wrongdoing and leave us without an answer to the question what to do; so then in the former case, the case of benevolence, common-sense morality may *provide too little* in answer to our practical perplexities. We may want to know whether our present lives can be justified and to what extent we ought to give to others, but common-sense morality may simply be unable to provide the full answer we crave.

Moreover, if consequentialism and common-sense morality both move towards scalar expression, the differences between them may come to seem less great than has initially been supposed. Common-sense morality loses, or partially loses, its advantage of combining validity with action-guiding force (or capacity) and both viewpoints seem to offer less complete guidance than their earlier proponents (e.g. Ross and Bentham) hoped for and, indeed, presupposed. (The scalar common-sense morality of benevolence might also, like traditional utilitarianism, suggest ways of supplementing itself with useful, though conventional and objectively non-valid, rules to settle issues where it could not itself do this.)

But the differences between the common-sense morality of actions and act-consequentialism nonetheless remain. The two may approach one another in the area of benevolence, where the consideration of consequences is common-sensically most prevalent. But even here our common-sense obligations of benevolence, i.e., what counts common-sensically as morally better or worse action with respect to benevolence, is contoured by considerations of agent-sacrifice and deontological agent side-constraints – though I have simplified the present discussion by ignoring all problems about how these interact with scalar benevolence. And certainly outside the area of benevolence, especially in those cases where the side-constraints themselves are most prominent, the divergence between scalar consequentialism and common-sense morality is considerable and highly visible.

One might wonder, of course, whether the two might possibly, of their own weight, be brought even closer together by showing that even the side-constraints on killing, maiming, deceiving, and the like might eventually best be understood in a scalar way. After all, most of those who believe in the side-constraints are willing to grant that they may cease to be in force in cases where ten, a hundred, or a million times more good can be done by violating them, and this very quantitativeness and the fact that different philosophers appear to have different intuitions about just how much achievable good allows us to override the side-constraints might possibly make one wonder whether the side-constraints should be thought of as a matter of degree and in a scalar way.[13] Such a scalar conception would indeed move common-sense morality closer, though still not all the way, to act-consequentialism. But since I have no very clear idea of what a scalar deontology would look like, much less any clear idea of how to defend such a thing, these few thoughts must remain for the moment mere moral speculations, gestures in a possible and possibly attractive direction. There are enough problems with the forms of scalar morality discussed in this chapter to occupy us for the moment.

VI

CONSEQUENTIALISM AND BEYOND

The last chapter explored some theoretical reasons for preferring scalar versions of both act-consequentialism and motive-consequentialism. But a certain dilemma arises for utilitarians and other consequentialists in connection with these different levels at which consequentialist moral judgments can be made, in connection, that is, with the different sorts of objects, or entities, that can be the subject of consequentialist moral evaluation. If one is both a motive-consequentialist and an act-consequentialist, for example, then there will be occasions when acting in accordance with a (generally) good (or the best) motive will produce less good than some other action and so count as wrong by the traditional act-consequentialist standard. It has long been recognized that such situations give rise to a certain sort of conflict,[1] and in the present chapter, I would like to discuss the possible implications of such conflicts for the further development of consequentialism. (The discussion will not, however, rely on what has been said in previous chapters about the defensibility of satisficing and scalar forms of consequentialism.)

1

Conflict between motive-consequentialism and act-consequentialism arises, in what is perhaps its most blatant form, in those cases where a given motive involves a certain disregard for consequentialist or utilitarian grounds. If love for one's spouse or children is a good 'motive' because its existence in people generally does so much good, then some motives that count as good in motive-consequentialist terms may nonetheless dictate wrong actions by any usual act-consequentialist standard. Thus a person who really loves his child will in some circumstances favour that child rather than perform an act that would do more good, impersonally considered. He will, for example, save his own child from drowning rather than save two, or several, others whom he does not know, and such a tendency to go against act-consequentialist optimality may actually be criterial, or definitional, of what it is to love someone. Yet such a tendency may have better long-run consequences than a love-precluding tendency always to prefer optimific actions, i.e., than a total and absorbing commitment to doing what is right by the act-consequentialist standard.

In the above example of drowning, the conflict between act- and motive-consequentialism appears as a conflict, for a given agent, between doing the right thing and acting from the morally best general motive. And one way of resolving the sense of conflict, in favour of doing a loving, rather than a right, action, would be to focus on the good consequences of the loving tendency that in this one case dictates a wrongdoing by the lights of act-consequentialism. If from an impersonal standpoint it is better on the whole that someone have the motive of love; if it is psychologically (or conceptually) impossible for someone who loves to abandon the loved one on occasions when he could do more good by doing so; if, that is, a more finely contoured motive than love which would prefer optimal consequences to the well-being of the loved one when these (glaringly) conflicted is simply psychologically impossible, then occasional wrong actions may simply be the price one has to pay for an overall better world history, and the consequentialist may feel he has no reason to flinch at the fact that love sometimes dictates acts that are wrong from an act-utilitarian or act-consequentialist standpoint. Since, to put the matter slightly differently,[2] the loving parent has no consequentialist reason to (try to) change his tendency to love, and indeed has the best consequentialist reasons for trying to preserve that tendency, we cannot as good consequentialists deplore or regret his *acting* upon that tendency. The conflict between motive- and act-consequentialism is thus (at least in this case) resolved in favour of (or at least not against) the agent's acting, as he predictably does, from love: his actions represent a necessary evil in the best achievable train of events, a case of *particular* wrongdoing with a *larger*, *overall* moral justification.

However, a question naturally arises as to whether an act-utilitarian or act-consequentialist *agent* can so sanguinely accept the fact that, on a given occasion, he has done or is about to do what he thinks is morally wrong, out of a generally good motive. Isn't it part of commitment to an act-morality that one regret or feel remorse about failure to live up to its dictates? One's answer to that question will depend, in part, on one's attitude towards the familiar 'overridingness thesis' according to which one can never be justified (overall) in doing a morally wrong action and according to which (to put the matter moral-psychologically) a moral individual is never willing, in the long run, to stand by an act whose wrongness she acknowledges. I have in *Goods and Virtues* argued for the possibility of cases in which someone with a general commitment to morality might be willing nonetheless to stand by wrongdoing or feel justified in acting wrongly, without even having the sort of presumptive overall moral justification that can be invoked in favour of the person who acts wrongly from an optimific motive.[3] And the consequentialist might think to take sustenance from such cases by claiming that there is *all the more reason* to speak of an overall justification for a particular wrongdoing when that wrongdoing is dictated by a motive that *can* be given a moral justification. So it might seem that a person who loved his children but (insofar as this was possible) had a belief in and commitment to the ethics of consequentialism could justify his giving preference to his own child not merely in personal, but in moral terms, that he could, in consonance with his own consequentialist moral motivation, feel justified, morally justified, in doing something that act-consequentialism deems to be wrong.

I think, however, that very serious doubts can be raised as to whether such a justification really is available to the (imperfectly) consequentialist moral agent. As I have indicated, the objection is not that the idea that one can be (feel) justified in doing wrong is inconsistent with a proper acknowledgment of the importance of (seriousness of) morality. Nor is my objection based on what might at first be thought to be a failure, on the part of those who claim an overall consequentialist justification for certain particular wrongdoings, to recognize the element of (free) choice by which, say, a parent decides to help his own child rather than others. From the fact (if it is a fact) that it is not causally (or conceptually) possible that a parent love his child and not give him some sort of preference (in certain circumstances), it does not obviously follow that such a parent acts unfreely, without genuine alternatives, when he acts to save his own child rather than others. But those who have sought to justify that loving parent's behaviour in consequentialist terms have not always failed to recognize that such behaviour is in no way obviously unfree or lacking in alternatives for the agent.[4]

However, once such assumptions about the agent's freedom are held firmly in view, I believe it becomes *more difficult* to argue for the agent's overall moral justification in consequentialist moral terms, and my reasons for saying so are initially perhaps most forcefully presented in terms of what might be going on in an agent who had generally consequentialist motivation, but loved his child, and was faced with a decision as to whether to save his child in preference to several other people. (I shall assume that such an agent is at least enough of a moral consequentialist to be willing to consider, and consider in moral terms, whether to rescue his own child. But this assumption would not hold for most parents, as Bernard Williams has made very clear.)[5]

The parent caught between the 'dictates' of love and the demands of his own act-consequentialism may well be swayed by love into a decision to give preference to his own child, and he may well feel justified, and continue to feel justified, in so acting. But the question before us is whether that justification can count, in consequentialist terms, as a moral justification or whether any justification he may have in acting from love may not better be conceived as non-moral or even contra-moral, i.e., as a distinctively consequentialist version of the sort of contra-moral justification discussed, with the aid of numerous examples, in *Goods and Virtues*.

My main reason for suggesting this possibility stems from what act-consequentialists and others have said about the fundamental moral motivation behind act-consequentialism and consequentialism generally. It has increasingly become a matter of agreement between consequentialists and anti-consequentialists alike that the most fundamental consequentialist motivation is a concern for how things turn out in the world, a concern that, from a long-range and impersonal standpoint, things should turn out for the best (or well).[6] This fundamental concern explains why act-consequentialists sometimes say that their own doctrine should not be recommended to people if the long-run results of doing so would be worse than leaving them uninitiated. And it also makes it easy to see how motive-consequentialism might appear attractive. If a better long-run course of events will be achieved if certain motives exist, then those motives can be recommended in consequentialist terms even if they bring occasional wrong actions in their wake.

I have no intention of disputing the existence of a consequentialist justification for certain motives, like love, which may occasionally bring non-optimific actions in their wake. But those act-consequentialists who defend the loving parent's saving his own child are seeking to give a consequentialist moral justification not only to the general motive from which he acts, but to the specific act of giving preference to his child; they are saying that this act, which they themselves acknowledge to be wrong, is morally justified because of the kind of moral justification its motive has. And I think in fact that it is very difficult to make sense of this transference of moral justification from a motive to actions it motivates, in consequentialist terms. For in the situation where the loving father has to choose between giving preference to his own child or doing the optimific act, it is difficult to see how the former choice could possibly be justified in terms of the desire/ concern that things occur for the best. As the situation presents itself to the parent as agent, he has a choice between doing an act that benefits his child but results in less long-run good and doing precisely what will lead to the best long-run train of events, and even if his love for his child pulls him towards helping his child, he must surely acknowledge that helping the others is the only way to satisfy the desire for the best possible long-run history of things. Insofar as he loves, he may only imperfectly embody that fundamental consequentialist motivation, but in the circumstances in which he acts (and if he is at all clear-headed) it ought to be clear which act best serves and embodies that fundamental consequentialist motivation. So it is difficult to see how he could think that the giving of preference to his own child could be justified in the most fundamental consequentialist moral terms. To the extent he is a clear-headed consequentialist about morality, he will at best be able to claim a non-moral or contra-moral justification for giving preference to his own child.

Indeed, the problem with claiming that the loving father can be justified in consequentialist terms is very similar to a well-known difficulty with rule-utilitarianism. The latter (typically) tells us that one may be morally justified (and not be acting wrongly) in following certain generally optimific rules even when one could do more good by not following them, and act-utilitarians have pointed out how irrational such a view is from the utilitarian standpoint.[7] If rules are to be justified in terms of their long-run good consequences, then it is absurd to demand adherence to those rules when non-adherence would clearly produce better long-run consequences. Rule-utilitarianism thus makes the mistake of supposing that since the general practice of having certain rules is morally justifiable in consequentialist terms, every application of those rules is also justified in those terms. And so it turns out that what fundamentally grounds rule-utilitarianism, the fundamental moral concern that things turn out as well as possible, itself helps to cut the ground from under rule-utilitarianism.

The attempt to produce a consequentialist moral justification for acting non-optimifically from a generally optimific motive seems as doomed to failure as the attempt to give a consequentialist moral justification for rule-utilitarianism. If one is interested in (concerned with) things turning out as well as possible, then one will ultimately be as little concerned with whether a certain act is dictated by an optimific motive as with whether a given act is dictated by an optimific rule. One's basic concern will be with what, then and there, one can do to affect how well things turn out, and so, just as fundamental consequentialist motivation dictates that one is not (morally) justified in following a rule when one can achieve a better overall result by breaking it, so too, in the case of love, will such motivation dictate that one is not (morally) justified in acting out of love when better overall results could be achieved by one's acting otherwise. And if it seems odd to suppose that there might sometimes be no consequentialist moral justification for acting from a consequentialistically justified motive, the analogy with rules may help us see that what is thus odd is nonetheless, from a consequentialist standpoint, distinctly possible. (What may also help is the distinction, familiar from debates about nuclear deterrence, between the usefulness, or moral justifiability, of an intention to retaliate and the usefulness, or moral justifiability, of actually acting on that intention.)[8]

Thus when the parent of our example is deciding whether to help his child or several others, it may be quite clear in consequentialist terms that it would be wrong for him to (try to) get rid of his love for his child; and to that degree, there may be a consequentialist moral justification for (his continuing to have) his motive of love. But just as the issue whether (it is right) to help his child is different, for the consequentialist, from the question whether (it is right) to keep loving the child, the issue of ultimate consequentialist justification for helping the child is different from the issue of ultimate consequentialist moral justification for retaining the love. The existence of a moral justification for not getting rid of the love may show something about the moral justifiability of that motive, but appears to prove nothing whatever about the consequentialist moral defensibility of the non-optimific act of saving the child (out of love).[9]

As I have been suggesting, however, this failure of consequentialist moral justification may not leave the loving parent without any justification for (the act of) saving his own child. Even acknowledging the absence of a (consequentialist) moral justification for what he does, the person who believes in and normally adheres to (act-)consequentialist morality may nonetheless be willing to stand by what he has done, and in this respect he is in the same position as the sort of common-sense-morality-assuming father described in *Goods and Virtues*, who is willing to stand by (and believes he is on the whole justified in regard to) an act of lying to the police in order to save his son from just arrest for a crime the son is in fact guilty of. Such a father feels he mustn't let the police find his son, but must, instead, do everything in his power to help him get to a place of safety, even though he is also willing to admit that there can be no *moral* justification for what he is doing. And indeed parental love can lead a parent (though not necessarily every loving parent) to act this way and allow him to feel justified in doing so. But even if, in common-sense moral terms, it can sometimes be right to give preference to members of one's own family (to save one's child in preference to a group of others) and can sometimes be right to lie to someone bent on harm, valid common-sense morality cannot reasonably be thought to include a principle allowing one to lie to legitimate authorities in order to save a guilty offspring. More importantly, there is no reason to deny that the devoted father of this example sincerely believes that the moral injunction against lying allows no exception in the case at hand. The cause in which he acts is sufficiently important from his own standpoint that one can see how it might outweigh something else that *really counted with him*. So the fact that such a father opts against morality and is willing to stand by what he has done cannot plausibly be taken to show that his previous concern for (the) morality (of truthtelling) wasn't genuine. In this case, then, personal considerations override (for a given individual) the (believed) fact of immorality, and we seem to have an example, then, of extramoral justification for what is in common-sense terms a wrong action. Moreover, for reasons too complicated to enter into, but explored at some length in *Goods and Virtues*, the common-sensically moral father cannot relevantly be said to have some larger or overall moral justification for his admittedly wrong action. So relative to common-sense moral assumptions, there may be such a thing as justified immoral action, or at least action that the common-sense moral agent conceives as wrong but is nonetheless, in the long term, willing to stand by. And what I have been suggesting about the consequentialist moral position is that it too may wish to make room for the possibility of justified actions that are nonetheless not morally justified, not justified in consequentialist moral terms. The case of the consequentialist agent who saves his own son from drowning may best be seen, not as a case where in terms of the consequentialist morality of motives he is morally justified in doing wrong, but rather as a case where he may be justified in personal, extramoral terms in doing a wrong act that is simply incapable of being given any larger *moral* justification. And the similarity of such a case to that of the father who lies to authorities helps to make clear how the possibility of extramorally justified immorality can exist in relation both to consequentialist and to common-sense moral assumptions (theories).

2

We have seen, then, that a parent having to decide between saving his own child and some optimific different act will have to acknowledge the consequentialist moral unjustifiability of acting to save his child. From his perspective as an agent, the only available act that serves the fundamental consequentialist concern for things to turn out as well as possible is the act that produces the most overall good and that act alone can be given a fundamental consequentialist moral justification in his circumstances. But *this* conclusion about justification is clearly not limited to the perspective of the agent trying to decide what to do in the situation we have described. Utilitarianism and consequentialism are (most) appealing when we step back from our roles as agents and consider, in impersonal detachment from our particular identities, what we would like to see happen. But someone with perfect consequentialist motivation, considering the situation of our loving parent from an impersonal standpoint, would presumably wish for that parent to perform the optimific act, rather than help his own child. Not being subject to the parent's particular attachment to his child, such an impersonal consequentialist observer would presumably have no desire to see the father save his child; he would lack the father's ambivalence about how to act and at the time when the father was deciding what to do would simply and unequivocally root for him to do the optimific thing. The attitude of such an observer makes even clearer the difficulty of giving a consequentialist moral justification for the parent's saving his own child. Given his detached consequentialist standpoint and his purely consequentialist motivation, he cannot want the father to favour his own child, cannot want him to do what would be wrong in act-consequentialist terms. Thus from the standpoint of an agent having to decide what to do at a given time, or of anyone observing that agent who can empathize (either before or after the fact) with his problem of decision and share, in that degree, his agential temporal standpoint, putative conflicts between motive-consequentialism and act-consequentialism must always, I think, be decided in favour of the latter – on the assumption of purely consequentialist moral motivation. One cannot be justified, in purely consequentialist terms, in doing a wrong act that is dictated by a generally good, or best, motive.

But consequentialism typically involves not only the assumption that the fundamental moral motivation is the desire/concern that things turn out for the best but also a particular view about the point of view from which such motivation is most reasonably applied in (or to) the making of moral judgments. Consequentialism typically assumes that moral truth is best understood if one takes an impersonal standpoint, if one gets outside of oneself and views oneself, others and the universe as a whole from a point of view, as it were, outside the universe. One is supposed to arrive at the correct view of right action and good motives if one adopts such an impersonal or detached standpoint and considers what actions and what motives would be preferred from such a standpoint, given the fundamental concern that things should turn out as well as possible.

Now consequentialists have emphasized the importance, for the ultimate justification of moral judgments, of one particular form of detachment from our normal role as agents within the world. Moral judgments are, they hold, best made from a standpoint that abstracts from the identity or individuality of the agent, from a standpoint that detaches us from identity with any particular agent and takes us outside the world altogether. But such impersonality is not the only sort of detachment from our normal roles and character that can be imagined. Someone who imaginatively abstracts himself from his own identity and places himself above or outside the universe may nonetheless occupy such an impersonal perspective at an (imagined) particular time. He may view the events of the world and the doings of himself and other agents from a point spatially outside the world, yet still regard the world as a whole and the agents in it from a temporal viewpoint held in common with people *in* the world, imaginatively sharing a sense of what is present, past, or future, with those he impersonally observes. And it is worth noting that the above-mentioned impersonal observer of the loving parent was treated as at least imaginatively sharing with the latter the sort of temporal perspective or location from which or at which the issue of whether to perform one action or another can arise for an agent.

But there is some tradition in the idea that the proper perspective from which to make and justify consequentialist moral judgments is a perspective freed not only from personal identity and spatial location but from temporal location as well. On such a view, the endemic consequentialist drive for impersonality carries along with it a drive for an atemporal total view of the universe, and the fundamental concern that things turn out well is best expressed in moral judgments via the perspective of a *sub specie aeternitatis* (impersonal) view of things.[10] Now our earlier arguments for the conclusion that, from a consequentialist perspective, the loving parent acts in a morally unjustifiable way when he saves his own child assumed the perspective of an agent deciding what to do or an impersonal observer sharing the temporal perspective of such an agent. But if an atemporal *sub specie aeternitatis* viewpoint is the proper one from which to make and justify consequentialist moral judgments, if there is something less than ideal, in consequentialist terms, about an impersonal but temporal moral perspective, then there may be a way to reopen the issue of the moral justification of the loving parent, and in what follows, I shall explore how this might be done.

3

The above-discussed conflict between motive-consequentialism and act-consequentialism could not exist but for the fact that act-consequentialism and motive-consequentialism are separate moral theories. Motive-utilitarianism and motive-consequentialism generally evaluate motives in separation from actions. Motives and more complex patterns of motivation are compared with one another in terms of their respective consequences, but there is no comparison between motives and *acts* in terms of their respective consequences and indeed one who accepts motive consequentialism is not thereby committed to any evaluation whatever of actions. By the same token, an act-consequentialist morally evaluates actions in terms of their respective consequences and as such makes no comparisons between the effects of motives and the effects of acts and no evaluations whatever of motives. Theories like act-consequentialism and motive-consequentialism are what Sen has called 'single influence' forms of consequentialism, and even when two or more such forms of consequentialism are held simultaneously (as, for example, when one holds what Adams calls motive-and-act consequentialism) the evaluation of acts and of motives (or whatever else) are kept in isolation within the total theory; there is no attempt to apply some consistent set of evaluations to different patterns of action-cum-motivation.[11]

But consider what happens if one assumes an impersonal *sub specie aeternitatis* view of what occurs over time in the world.

Does one from such a perspective, and given a concern that things turn out for the best, have any reason to evaluate actions in separation from motives, traits of character, etc., in the manner of act-consequentialism? Indeed, will such a perspective not naturally generate the very opposite of single influence theories, namely, comprehensive moral theories that compare and evaluate total combinations of those consequence-influencing factors in agents that are evaluated singly in such theories as motive-utilitarianism and act-utilitarianism? Someone viewing the world from such a perspective has no reason to pick out particular actions for evaluation rather than total sequences of action, and no reason to evaluate total sequences of actions in separation from those other factors, like motivation and dispositions, that also bear on how well things turn out on the whole. Rather, from such a perspective, given consequentialist motivation, the kind of consequentialist theory that seems most naturally generated is one that evaluates and compares total combinations of consequence-influencing agent variables and that says, e.g., that one (transpersonal and transtemporal) total pattern of motives, acts, traits, and dispositions is better than another if it produces more good on the whole than that other.[12] And once such a theory is generated, there is no need or reason from an atemporal impersonal perspective to generate, in addition, the sort of single influence theories that have been the stock in trade of previous consequentialism.

But the conflict between motive- and act-consequentialism we discussed earlier arises because of their independent evaluations of motives and actions; once one evaluates motives in combination with actions and other consequence-influencing agent factors, one can presumably produce a consistent evaluation in which that earlier conflict dissolves or disappears. A comprehensive or total-influence theory of the sort just mentioned might well say, for example, that the combination of our parent's loving his child and saving him and doing the various other things such a parent can be supposed to do (together with all other agent factors over time in the world) was productive of better consequences than any other physically and psychologically possible total combination of agent factors, and as such that combination would presumably qualify as good or right according to that comprehensive total-influence theory.[13] But then in the absence of a single influence act-consequentialist theory that questioned the rightness of what the father did, and thus provided a way of questioning the justifiability of his behaviour, the fact that a more comprehensive consequentialist moral theory included such action in the total combination of factors it considered morally best (or good enough) might well be all the moral justification such behaviour could need or require, all, at least, that needed to be said in its favour. The justification of what the father does from love may thus, from a consequentialist standpoint, be best achieved by outflanking act-consequentialism rather than confronting it directly. If the atemporal standpoint is *the* proper one for consequentialist moral evaluation and if such a standpoint naturally generates total-influence theories rather than single or less-than-total-influence theories, then act-consequentialism and other single-influence theories may themselves have every reason to fade from the consequentialist-theoretic scene, superseded by the more comprehensive theories that the consequentialist moral standpoint naturally favours. The act of the loving father may then be as justified as it needs to be, in purely consequentialist moral terms. And since we are now accepting the idea that consequentialist moral theory need not aspire to a role in the practical regulation of action, there is no reason to try to reinstate act-consequentialism by insisting that the atemporal impersonal moral perspective must (somehow) leave room for and give rise to single influence theories like act-consequentialism that are more practical or more practically relevant than comprehensive theories. Morever, Sen has pointed out that any single influence theory allows for slippage between what it holds to be morally good or best and the best possible resultant total history of events.[14] And such slippage is yet another (and perhaps even a stronger) reason for supposing that the consequentialist concern for the best history of things when wedded to a *sub specie aeternitatis* view of things has no reason to generate anything but comprehensive total-influence forms of consequentialism. (Such theories, obviously, can be held in optimizing, satisficing or scalar form.)

The upshot of the present discussion, then, is that we must choose between disallowing the sort of justification for doing what act-consequentialism deems to be wrong that certain consequentialists have tried to give and disallowing act-consequentialism itself. In neither case will consequentialism be able to give a theoretical justification of the idea of a morally justified but morally wrong action, but if, as I tend to assume, we decide to leave act-consequentialism behind and adopt more comprehensive views, something like a moral justification for certain acts act-consequentialism deems wrong will in fact be forthcoming. The parent who favours his own child will not seem morally unjustified (not seem lacking in moral justification for what he does), but neither, on the other hand, will we want to characterize what he does as a case of morally justified wrongdoing. (Of course, if we wish, instead, to leave room for a temporally located impersonal consequentialist standpoint and for act-consequentialism as a distinct theory, the father's saving his own child can at best be given a contra-moral justification.)

Assuming, however, that an atemporal perspective is to be the fundamental basis for moral evaluations, are even total-influence consequentialist theories capable of surviving and remaining justified? Having discarded single-influence moral theories, we must now consider whether (scalar, optimizing or satisficing) total-influence theories are the most natural theoretical expression of the favoured consequentialist perspective. What worries me here, in particular, is the question of what motivation, if any, there can be for theories that evaluate total historical patterns of *agent*-variables in terms of how they affect the goodness of total world histories. Total-influence theories focus on factors and combinations of factors within agents or groups of agents, and evaluate such total combinations in terms of how they causally affect total histories of things. But we may well ask why someone with the consequentialist concern that things turn out for the best should from the impersonal standpoint of all eternity have reason to evaluate total patterns of agent-factors in terms of whether they lead to (or underlie) good or best total world histories *rather than simply, and more directly, evaluating those total world histories*. Why should such a hypothetical being, even given his benign moral motivation, care about cutting up the world into an agent-part producing good consequences and the (partly overlapping) total good consequences thereby produced? Why should he have (or be interested in) a consequentialist morality of agent-factors (whether single-influence or total-influence) *in addition* to (what Sen has called) an 'outcome morality' that evaluates total histories for their goodness. Once consequentialism allows itself to cut away the practical character of valid morality (moral theory) and once we presuppose the favoured atemporal perspective, it is hard to see how to justify having a morality that separately evaluates agent-factors, a separate 'agent-morality'. We are given no particular moral or theoretical motivation either for single-influence agent-moralities like act-consequentialism or for total influence consequentialist agent-moralities of the sort mentioned just above, and in that case consequentialism as a moral view involving the evaluation of agent-factors in terms of the impersonal goodness of their consequences, consequentialism as a moral view involving two evaluated factors related as cause and effect, consequentialism as a moral view about *consequences* may just possibly end up by swallowing its own tail. In the end, we may be left on consequentialist theoretical grounds with a (scalar) 'outcome morality' that has no claim to be called a form of consequentialism – or even, speaking literally, a morality.[15] This is obviously a conclusion that the consequentialist will want, and have reason, to resist. But in order to do so, I think he will need either to find some plausible justification for not theoretically ascending to the timeless standpoint at which single-influence forms of consequentialism seem to fade away or else to explain how that timeless standpoint can possibly recommend the excision of total historical patterns of agent-factors from possible overall histories of the world and a separate evaluation of such patterns in terms of their contribution to the total goodness of those histories.

VII

COMMON-SENSE MORALITY
AND THE FUTURE

Having just explored some problems for consequentialism as a moral theory, I would next like to consider some difficulties of common-sense morality that have not previously been mentioned. All along, we have proceeded by comparing common-sense morality and consequentialism with one another, and these comparisons have, I believe, not only helped us to a better understanding of the nature and implications of these two major kinds of substantive moral theory, but have also underscored, and in some cases uncovered, major problems in each theory. In Chapter I, for example, we discussed a number of difficulties that common-sense morality faces because it pays less attention to good consequences than consequentialism does. As Nozick, Nagel and Scheffler have noted, it is very difficult to get a good intellectual grip on, much less justify, the deontological side-constraints or restrictions of common-sense morality once one sees them as limitations on the permissibility of producing optimal consequences. And we also saw in Chapter I that our common-sense deontological side-constraints involve a self-other asymmetry which is difficult to understand or justify quite apart from all the other difficulties with the side-constraints.

But if the side-constraints can be criticized, from a consequentialist standpoint, as giving insufficient moral weight to consequences, common-sense morality is in other areas open to the precisely opposite charge that it pays too much attention to consequences. Ordinary moral thinking distinguishes the moral status of attempted murder from that of murder, for example, and although this distinction is exemplified in legal distinctions between the status and punishability of murder and attempted murder, its moral significance is by no means exhausted by the role it plays in specifically legal contexts. Thus quite apart from legal differences between murder and attempted murder, we think much worse of someone who has killed an innocent victim than of someone who accidentally fails to kill an intended innocent victim. We think much worse of him and of what he has done, and these differences can be seen in our inclination to heap greater blame upon an actual murderer (for what he has done) than we do upon an unsuccessful one and also, I imagine, in the greater revulsion we feel in confronting (knowingly sitting next to) a murderer than in confronting (knowingly sitting next to) someone who has merely attempted murder.

To the extent that common-sense morality accepts and encourages these differences of feeling and moral judgment, it allows actual unforeseeable consequences a role in determining moral judgment, thus making room for a certain kind of 'moral luck'. And as has been frequently pointed out, the idea of moral luck affronts our common-sense moral intuitions. So our moral intuitions about cases taken singly are in conflict with a general common-sense moral conviction that judgments of morally better and worse, or greater or less culpability or blameworthiness, cannot properly be subject to luck or accident. And this conflict, which goes extremely deep in our ordinary moral view of things and is very difficult to resolve or undercut in any satisfactory way, represents yet another difficulty for the defender of common-sense morality.

Of course, consequentialism also involves single judgments which, taken together, entail the possibility of moral luck. To the extent that rightness and wrongness depend on consequences and consequences are frequently a matter of luck or accident, the maximizing, optimizing, satisficing or scalar consequentialist must admit the possibility of moral luck with regard both to actions and motives (or other agent-factors), and, as I said, such luck offends against the strong common-sense moral conviction that morality must not, cannot, be subject to luck or accident. (Consequentialists often seek to palliate these consequences of their theory by holding that one may be morally to blame for acts that are in fact morally right.) However, since consequentialism in other respects and in other areas knowingly offends against common-sense intuitions, since consequentialism does not seek to measure its own success or validity by a common-sense moral yardstick, the consequentialist may not be as bothered by his commitment to moral luck as the defender of common-sense morality ought to be. The difficulties raised by moral luck — unlike, e.g., at least some of the well-known criticisms of side-constraints — are difficulties that arise from within the perspective of common-sense morality itself. They cannot be dismissed by invoking the intuitiveness of what is being criticized, since in the phenomenon of moral luck ordinary intuition itself is shown to yield inconsistencies.

Moral luck, then, raises greater problems for, or from the perspective of, common-sense morality than for, or from the perspective of, consequentialism. And it is not clear how the defender of common-sense morality, or, indeed, anyone seeking to understand the rationale behind ordinary moral thinking should respond to this whole phenomenon. In this present, final chapter, I shall argue, however, that we can at least get a better sense of what is at stake in certain forms of moral luck, by placing that issue in a wider context of related problems. The kind of moral luck that arises in connection with actions and their consequences is, I want to argue, just one example of a phenomenon I shall call 'covert relationality'. And once we have characterized covert relationality and seen the variety of its instances, we shall be able better to understand and account for not only moral luck but a related moral phenomenon that our common-sense morality also, arguably, makes room for: the possibility that the rightness or wrongness of a given action can in part depend on what its agent does in the future, i.e., subsequently.

1

Consider – the example is borrowed from Sartre – what seems to be involved in an aspiring author's having, at a given time, or over a period of time, a profound comprehension of his own worth or value. Such self-comprehension appears at first glance to involve certain facts about the person at the time(s) in question and perhaps also some suppositions about the past processes whereby he came to believe in his own value. Certainly no predictions about the future seem to be at issue. And yet it turns out that the future is involved. An aspiring writer counts as having a profound comprehension of his own worth as a writer only if he later produces books commensurate with that earlier self-estimation.[1] Nothing else will do, and this claim involves no blurring of epistemic and metaphysical modalities. I am not (merely) saying that we can only *know* whether a young artist's sense of his own value is correct or justified by waiting and seeing what he later produces; I am saying that whether or not a young writer counts, at a given time, as having a profound comprehension of (as distinct from belief in) his own worth as an artist depends on what he will actually do in the future; and yet I agree that this dependence on future events is hardly obvious. The predicate 'has a profound comprehension of his own worth' seems to refer to a present worth and present comprehension and to have no reference to the (distant) future, so if its applicability turns out to depend on the future in the way I have claimed, we shall have a good example of what I mean by covert (temporal) relationality.

But are we really unable to imagine someone having profound comprehension of his own worth as a writer and yet somehow failing to write any good books? Certainly even writers with great potential may somehow fail to realize the talents or gifts they may (undeniably) have. And yet talent and gifts are, I think, for that very reason different from what we are talking about. A talent, like any potential for doing something, is inherently liable to failure or non-fulfilment, through unfavourable circumstances or even bad luck. And since we can imagine cases where a person's fulfilment of earlier promise hinges on a chance encounter or a fortuitous relationship, it is even possible to imagine someone with great talent ending up doing nothing but mediocre work. But the notion of having a profound comprehension of one's own worth as a writer is not like attributions of talent in this respect: it is not a merely dispositional notion; it ascribes more than an ability. And I think the clearest indication of this is our reluctance to use this notion of a (possible or imagined) individual who fails to fulfil his early promise. One may, for example, write a story of a young scientist who had every talent imaginable, but through an unfortunate series of accidents failed to realize his potential. But it would be extremely odd to write, even in the omniscient third person, of a young scientist who had a profound comprehen-

110

sion of his own worth as a scientist, but through an unfortunate series of accidents altogether failed to make any great or interesting discoveries. A story will simply not describe someone as having at a given time a profound comprehension of his own worth unless it also at some point says (or implies) that the person in question at some time achieves excellence.

If what I have been suggesting, then, is correct, an aspiring scientist or writer has a profound comprehension of his own value only if the prediction or claim that he will do valuable work in the future is, or comes, true. But to say that a certain prediction will come true is to make a claim clearly and obviously about the future, whereas the statement that someone has a profound comprehension of his own value at best involves only a covert reference to what will happen later. So at this point I imagine there must still be an air of paradox about what I am saying. Although evidence concerning linguistic usage points to a future reference in the predicate 'has a profound comprehension . . .', that phrase itself shows no sign of shedding the appearance of lacking such implications (unlike 'knows he will eventually do valuable work', which wears its temporal relationality practically on its face). Nor does it help much to point out that the future reference of 'has a profound comprehension . . .' is circumstantial or conditional. I am certainly not claiming that this predicate can never apply unless future achievements are in the offing, since what is simply described as a profound comprehension of one's own value may easily be based in achievements that are entirely past or present. But where someone has *not yet* achieved anything of note, he can correctly be described as having such comprehension only if he actually will do things in the future. In such circumstances, whether a person at a given time has profound comprehension depends on events subsequent to that time;[2] yet on the face of it, profound comprehension of one's worth seems entirely a matter of what is and has been, and so incapable of ever depending in this way on later developments. And it is this appearance of non-relationality that may make us doubt whether the application conditions of 'has a profound comprehension . . .' can be established by an appeal to common linguistic usage.

What might perhaps help the case for covert temporal relationality in the present instance would be some indication that what we have been investigating is not an isolated, bizarre example that can be summarily dismissed, but a puzzling yet widespread phenomenon. There are a great many examples of predicates which persistently *seem* to lack temporal relationality of one kind or another and yet whose conditions of application, as judged from our own tendencies to apply or withhold them, involve precisely such relationality. And once we become familiar with some of these cases, it may become easier to believe that, despite initial and indeed persistent appearances, the application of 'has a profound comprehension of his own value as a writer (scientist)' to a person at a time can depend on facts about what that person does later.

In some of the most fascinating of these other cases the very existence of a certain kind of thing at a time depends on what occurs after, even considerably after, that time. Thus whether a republic (has been founded and) exists at a certain time in a certain territory would seem to be a matter of what exists in that territory at that time and perhaps also of those essential factors in the past that may be involved in getting the republic into being in the first place. Surely, one thinks, nothing that happens later than a given time can be needed to propel a republic into being at that earlier time (I assume an absence of backwards causation), and to say that a republic depends for its existence at a particular time on what happens later than that time would appear to be like saying, e.g., of the American Republic that its *present* existence depends on whether a nuclear holocaust occurs in the *next few days*.

However, let us look more closely at the actual history of the American Republic. No future nuclear holocaust can undo the fact that it has already been founded and existed a long time, but that founding is itself rather problematic and in fact raises the issue of covert temporal relationality. When those serious and hopeful men met in Philadelphia during the spring and summer of 1776 and framed the Declaration of Independence, they founded a republic whose origin dates from that time. Yet the very existence of that republic (at that time) depended on what happened subsequently. If the revolution had not succeeded, the annals of history would have recorded a rebellion, but no new republic.

The issue here appears to be one of existence, not of reasonable beliefs about or knowledge of existence. It would be fairly implausible to claim, for example, that if the British had beaten back the rebellion, then there would have *been* a new republic between 4 July 1776, and the final defeat of the rebellion; only no one would have *known* of its existence. For in similar cases where rebellions have actually failed, the disinterested historian (as opposed, perhaps, to partisans of the rebellions) does not in fact claim that a new republic existed for a time. Perhaps history is made by victors, not the vanquished; but the historian may perhaps properly see in this fact not (only) some inevitable bias of all written histories, but (also) a reflection of his own reasonable practice of counting nations in accordance with principles that make the issue of whether a self-proclaimed republic is ever to count among the world's nations depend on its success in freeing itself from some previous hegemony. And since such a practice is commonplace and fairly uncontroversial, it lends support to our contention that the American Republic's existence from 4 July 1776 depends on the later success of the rebellion against the English.[3]

On the other hand, it might be granted that a republic's exist-ence can depend on the success of attempts to throw off the hegemony of a ruling power, but nonetheless held that the foun-ding of such a republic would in the latter event date from the moment of victory over the former ruling power, rather than from some earlier moment of self-proclaimed freedom. This *may* be so; but it is not in fact the way such matters are commonly regarded, and I wish merely to point out that our own implicit opinions about the existence conditions of republics, as reflected in our speech dispositions, entail a surprising temporal relationality in the concept of a republic's existing at a time.[4] The existence of a republic at a time may not always depend on subsequent events; given the actual past, no future facts seem capable of undermining the present existence of the American Republic; but sometimes the original emergence of a republic would appear to hang upon events later than the very time at which that republic is being said to emerge.

There are also, however, cases of covert relationality involving the past. I have in mind here not merely those essentialist views which, by claiming, e.g., that human beings essentially derive from their particular parents, make the existence of certain entities at a time depend in possibly surprising ways on much earlier events occurring to earlier entities. I am thinking, rather, of cases where the existence at a time of a certain *type* of entity depends not, as with emergent republics, on subsequent developments, but rather, in a perhaps equally surprising way, on events prior to the time in question.

Thus consider the Temple of Dendur being transported by ship from Egypt to New York. Although the Temple has been dismantled for the voyage, we would not naturally regard it as having been destroyed by that act; rather, the Temple is in transit (or it is in storage in the hold of a ship).[5] But notice the difference it makes to the case if we imagine the very same stones accidentally coming together in the hold of a ship as ballast, never having formed parts of a single temple and not being intended for reassembly in New York, or else imagine that they have been taken directly from the quarry and are to be made into a temple in Richard Nixon's townhouse garden. In either of the latter circumstances there is no temple, in transit or otherwise, in the hold of the ship; at most there is a group of stones that *will* or (unbeknownst to everyone) *could* be put together to make a temple. And yet the only relevant difference from the actual Temple of Dendur seems to be the prior existence of the Temple and the plans for transporting it disassembled to New York. This prior material and social context, however, is precisely what here seems to make the difference between there being a temple in transit and no temple at all. So we have another plausible instance of covert temporal relationality; only this time the relationality is towards the past, not the future. (Contrast the predicate 'is a scar', whose relationality towards the past is relatively easy to recognize.)

On the other hand, with respect to each of the particular cases we have considered, I find myself at least somewhat uncertain about the attribution of covert relationality. Even after pointing up those linguistic intuitions that naturally lead to the conclusion that the existence of a republic at a given time can depend on what happens later, I find it difficult entirely to shake the contrary intuition that the existence of a republic at a given time logically *cannot* depend on what happens later, that 'republic' is some sort of 'intrinsic' predicate free of any sort of relationality towards the future. I think, indeed, that some such tug-of-war naturally emerges in all putative cases of covert relationality, but rather than attempt here to come to a final decision as to the existence of this phenomenon, I would rather at this point concentrate on how the idea of covert relationality can help us to a better understanding both of the important phenomenon of moral luck and of the fascinating possibility that the morality of a given action may depend on its agent's later actions.

2

Imagine someone driving a car along a country road and pointing out noteworthy sights to his passengers. As a result of his preoccupation, the car suddenly swerves to the middle of the road; fortunately there are no cars coming in the opposite direction and no accident occurs. However, in another scenario the person is similarly preoccupied, and because a truck happens to be coming, has a major accident. He is then responsible for a great deal of harm to others and would normally be accounted blameworthy or culpable in a way that (to a degree that) he would not be thought blameworthy or culpable in the first-mentioned case. Thus one familiar illustration of the possibility of moral luck, as described, for example, in Thomas Nagel's groundbreaking paper on the subject. But Nagel also points out that something in us revolts against the idea of moral luck, inclining us to the view that the driver must have the *same* degree of culpability in the two cases mentioned above. There is something repelling in the idea that one can be more or less culpable depending on events outside one's ken or control.[6]

Now Nagel devotes a good deal of discussion to the sources and underpinnings of our unwillingness (entirely) to accept moral luck; but he also says something – not a great deal, but something – about what lies behind our thinking when we unself-consciously make those common-sense judgments which (collectively) imply the existence of moral luck. In particular, he claims that in cases of negligence we multiply the constant mental fault (culpability) by the seriousness of the outcome in determining (degree of) overall culpability. This would certainly give us (or come close to giving us) the right results for the above cases of preoccupied driving, but such an explanation of why we assign differential culpability in those cases suffers from two problems, one of which Nagel himself acknowledges.

The problem Nagel mentions is the *limitedness* of such an explanation of moral luck. He points out that in some putative cases of moral luck factors outside the agent's control seem to make the difference between an overall *positive* and overall *negative* evaluation, and this sort of difference cannot be readily explained or understood in terms of the multiplicative model he suggests for cases of negligence. Nagel offers no way to understand the variability from positive to negative that sometimes characterizes moral-luck-type thinking, and indeed his failure to do so connects with what I take to be the other problem with his brief analysis of cases of negligence. With respect to such cases, he assumes that (inner) mental fault is thought constant and what varies, depending on luck and circumstances, is some sort of overall judgment about the agent's action. But I believe that even those faults which one would naturally tend to think of as mental and inner, and hence intrinsic, or not relational, are in fact sometimes subject to moral luck. And once this is recognized, there is a way of handling those cases where moral luck seems to make a difference to the 'sign' of an action, rendering it culpable or estimable, morally better or worse, depending on factors outside an agent's control. For in such cases, I shall argue, the seemingly inner can (in certain respects) vary from positive to negative depending on factors – typically later factors – that are outside the agent's control, and we can use this fact to explain why a total act can vary the same way. The kind of moral luck that arises in connection with the antecedents and consequences of actions is, I shall argue, pervaded by the covert temporal relationality that attaches both to overall attributions of culpability and estimability and to the lower-order or more specific claims in which such judgments are grounded.

Let me begin by reconsidering the driving cases mentioned at the beginning of the present section. It might seem that such cases differ only in external luck and results, and have a common inner or mental fault of negligence or carelessness. Now I have no intention of denying that something inner or mental is common to the two cases. In both the driver is preoccupied with the scenery, not paying attention to the road – notice the fairly neutral character, morally speaking, of these descriptions. What I want to question, however, is whether the presumptively inner is in all respects the same between the two cases. Is it really clear that the degree of negligence or carelessness (not just the degree of culpability for negligence, but the degree of negligence, or carelessness, itself) is the same in the two cases. I am not sure, but I would hate to make any case depend on a definite answer, one way or another, to that question. In the first place, there are other kinds of cases where common-sense or common usage quite clearly treats the putatively inner fault of negligence as subject to external factors, to luck. Thus consider a guest being entertained on an island who absolutely has to get back to the mainland that night. He wants to leave early in order to be sure of catching a ferry, but his host assures him that the last ferry is not until such and such hour and is very reliable. The guest is persuaded to stay later, but the last ferry subsequently has mechanical difficulties and cannot leave – it is the first time this has ever happened – and the guest cannot get back to the mainland. Surely in the circumstances we would say that the host had been negligent as a host; but if no breakdown had occurred, I think we would not regard the host as negligent at all. And if luck can make a difference to the attribution of negligence in this case, perhaps there is a difference of negligence in our two driving examples.

More significantly, I can think of at least one other seemingly inner mental characteristic that, intuitively, does vary between the two driving cases, and it is a characterization highly relevant to the culpability of the driver's inattention. Whatever we say about negligence, I think our view of the *stupidity* of the driver in not paying attention to the road clearly does depend on how things turn out.[7] If there is no accident, and no near-accident, no one will, upon hearing of what happened, think that the driver was very stupid to pay more attention to the landscape than to his driving; but if an accident occurs, it will be natural to think just that; and this difference in reaction to the two cases indicates, contrary to Nagel's view, a tendency on our part to let moral luck intrude upon the inner.

Clearly, though, such thinking involves treating stupidity as less purely inner or purely mental than it is sometimes thought to be,[8] and it involves the idea that stupidity has a covert relationality towards the future, covert because it is hard to believe that whether one is acting stupidly at a given time can depend on what happens later (as a matter of luck). It seems as if we should be able to insert some sort of probability estimate that will do proxy for later results, so that whether the man of our examples was stupid would depend on whether he was sufficiently aware of the likelihood of an accident and on how likely it actually was for an accident to follow his preoccupation with the scenery, judgments that are constant between the two cases and that might allow us to say he was stupid (or not stupid) in both cases to the same extent for paying attention to the scenery. But (following Nagel) I think that no such solution really squares with the moral judgments we make in the ordinary course of events, before we begin to worry about moral luck in a self-conscious way. I think no matter how constant one imagines the (awareness of) probability in the two situations, common-sense morality sees some difference both in the culpability of the agent and in his stupidity. Thus, even in cases of negligence and carelessness of the sort Nagel mentions, I do not think that we can always multiply constant mental fault by result to arrive at the judgments that belief in moral luck tends to lead us to. The mental fault itself may vary, and the alternative is to recognize that judgments of overall culpability or merit can depend on luck at least in part because the judgments of the 'inner' on which they are based – and I assume, e.g., that judgments of culpability typically rest on some specific fault like stupidity or negligence – are also based on luck. This may not take us very far in explaining why our overall moral attributions depend on luck, but at least it gives us a picture of what is happening in such cases, and it also suggests a way of understanding those cases where overall moral judgment shifts from positive to negative.

A sentry given reasonable orders to shoot strangers on sight may be unable to bring himself to kill an approaching pregnant woman and the toddler she has in tow. If she is as harmless as she appears, then he will be thought commendable for displaying flexibility in interpreting orders; but if, on the contrary, she subsequently does things to help the enemy, a positive word like 'flexible' will seem inappropriate and we shall presumably regard him as culpable for his gullibility: it will seem wrong of him to have disobeyed orders. Thus according to (at least some) ordinary moral thinking the merit or demerit of the sentry's letting the woman live depends on features of the situation not subject to his control or certain knowledge and is therefore in some degree a matter of luck. But the luck here seems to affect not only the overall or resultant moral evaluation of his actions but (some of) those lower-order judgments in which the former are grounded. What seems like flexibility, in the light of a certain train of events, may appear to be a case of gullibility in the context of another scenario; and a crucial difference is made by what happens after, and in consequence of, the sentry's failure to shoot on sight.[9] So although Nagel assumes and it might first seem quite plausible to assume that mental or inner characteristics like flexibility and gullibility characterize someone's actions in virtue of their intrinsic character, and in particular their sensitivity to probabilities available to the agent within a given situation, I believe our actual judgments in these matters can depend on (what we believe or imagine to be) events subsequent to the actions that an agent is said to be gullible or flexible, etc., for performing.

In that case, we can offer a uniform account both of what occurs in cases of negligence or carelessness and of those cases of actions under uncertainty, like that of the sentry, where moral luck judgments actually vary from positive to negative. In both sorts of cases, the overall judgments that vary as a result of moral luck are grounded in more specific judgments that also hinge upon luck. But although it is some sort of advantage to have a unified account of these matters (as compared, for example, with Nagel's brief and ungeneralizable speculations about judgments of negligence and carelessness), the picture offered here has one obvious disadvantage. By insisting that even lower-level moral judgments involve an element of dependency on what happens later, and on luck, we drive the ultimate paradox of moral luck deeper into our conceptual scheme and thereby raise even greater problems for ourselves. Reflective moral thinking finds repugnant the idea of culpability or wrongness due in part to luck; but our previous arguments, instead of somehow relieving the conflict between our unself-conscious ordinary judgments and our reflective sensibility, imply that the conflict is actually more widespread than has previously been suggested. In that case, there is a certain amount of theoretical pressure to deny what I have been saying and treat as illusory the appearance of luck in judgments of gullibility, stupidity, carelessness, and the like. (As we shall see later, the present account also suffers from an inability to handle *every form* of moral luck.)

What might, on the other hand, induce us to grant these ideas a stay of execution is the similarity between what I have suggested about flexibility, etc., and all the other cases we have mentioned where what seems intrinsic turns out, if we credit our linguistic dispositions, to depend on what happens later and to involve an element of luck. Thus even the claim that a republic exists in a certain territory at a certain time seems to depend on whether the advocates of that republic are lucky enough to ward off attempts to keep or regain control of that territory by its (previous) rulers. Of course, in this particular example, it seems to be a non-moral predicate that is subject to what happens later, and to luck, so perhaps it is easier to accept such an example than ethical ones where the moral quality of an agent in performing a certain action is deemed to be dependent on factors of luck outside his control. But it is not obvious that this is so. Is our intuition that existence at a time cannot depend on what comes (possibly through luck) after that time really any weaker, or easier to shake off, than the parallel conviction about moral characterization? I am not sure that it is.

Moreover, the congruence or similarity between the above-mentioned examples of moral luck and the cases of the American Republic and the Temple of Dendur makes it even harder, I think, to proclaim either kind of case entirely illusory. If we dismiss the common-sense judgments that imply moral luck, then we still have to decide what to do with the non-moral cases, and to dismiss *all* cases of what I have been calling covert temporal relationality would require a great deal more justification than we have at present. The sheer number and variety of such examples ought to give us pause and make us take them seriously until we have a better idea of how to deal with them. And this becomes particularly convincing when we recognize that the moral and non-moral examples are not as mutually separable and unrelated as we have been treating them.

If the American Revolution had failed, then the leaders of the rebellion could have been accused of treason; but seeing their actions as treasonous largely depends on the assumption that they were trying to subvert their country and on the assumption therefore that there was no 'New Republic' that their actions were faithful to and that could count as an alternative measure of their fidelity or treasonousness. If, on the other hand, a republic came into being in July 1776, it is harder, if not impossible, to see these men as traitors rather than patriots, and to the extent, therefore, that the existence of the republic depends on the success of the rebellion, the latter also has an important role in determining whether the rebellion's leaders can be viewed as traitors. So in the present case the legal/moral epithet 'treason' depends on what comes later (and on luck) in part because the seemingly neutral description 'republic' has a similar sort of dependency.[10] We see, then, that moral luck of the sort we have described is part of a more general phenomenon of covert temporal relationality wherein higher-order moral judgments subject to luck can depend on more specific ones that are similarly luck-prone and moral judgments dependent on luck can depend on apparently non-moral attributions that depend on luck and on what happens later. But within the common-sense moral sphere there are also cases where the dependence of moral characterization on what happens later does not primarily involve luck, and we have so far held back from mentioning these. Covert temporal relationality occurs within the sphere of ordinary morality not only in those cases where the moral or ethical characterization of an action depends on later events outside an agent's control, but also in cases where the moral characterization of an earlier action depends on the actions that its agent, not through luck or accident but as a result of his own, free deliberations, performs later on.

3

The possibility that the moral characterization of an agent's action at one time may depend on the subsequent actions of that agent has recently been explored by Holly Goldman and J. Howard Sobel.[11] I shall not, however, enter into the details of their views, because their rather similar approaches are subject to telling critic-isms that Goldman herself has presented. As a result of those criticisms, Goldman goes on to conclude that 'the acts an agent would [later] perform if he performed a given act are not to be counted as relevant circumstances in assessing the moral status of that act'. But this conclusion is, I believe, premature. The approach of Goldman or Sobel may not allow us to vindicate the idea that later acts can affect the moral status of earlier ones, but I believe a quite different approach can be used at least to revive that idea for us, one making use of the notion of covert relationality and of examples quite different from any discussed by Goldman or Sobel.

Consider a couple who are living together: the man wants to get married, but the woman has no desire to do so – perhaps she feels he is not the sort of person she would want to spend her whole life with. One night, in a festive – though not necessarily drunken – mood, the woman proposes marriage to the man, promising to marry him at the appropriate government office during the coming week. She makes her promise (proposal) on the spur of the moment, but she presents it in a non-jocular fashion as a serious promise.

Now from the standpoint of prudence, such a spur-of-the-moment proposal seems ill-considered, even foolish. But it is also natural to wonder (with respect to any actual case of the above sort) whether the woman will actually go through with what she has promised, if and when, in the cold light of the next day, she decides that marriage with the man is not really what she wants.[12] Will she not perhaps refuse in the end to marry him even if this means cruelly disappointing him and probably wrecking their relationship? In the light of such possibilities, we are perhaps prepared to hold that if the woman doesn't carry through on her promise, she should never have made it in the first place – the 'should' here representing a claim of morality, not (merely) of prudence.

Now certain sorts of cases where it is in common-sense terms wrong to have promised at all are already familiar in the literature of ethics. If I have promised x to do y, at t, I shouldn't subsequently promise u to do some action v incompatible with y, at t. If I do so, then it is wrong of me to do so (I assume rather simple background circumstances to make this point; the examples and my conclusions here about them can be made more complicated). Similarly, if (in normal sorts of circumstances) I know that a situation is likely to arise in which any promise I now make will be overridden, then if I make a blanket promise to do something, I do something I shouldn't do. One is not (usually) morally free to promise when (one knows) one is not (going to be) morally free to *do* what one has promised.

Now the two just-mentioned instances of morally criticizable promising differ from the case of the woman who promises to marry the man she lives with, because in the latter any wrongness in the promising presumably cannot derive from the wrongness, in the particular situation, of fulfilling the promise. In fact, if the woman of our example does not do what she promised, we are likely to fault her both for making the promise in the first place and for not keeping the promise once made; but we are *more likely* to fault her (and fault her more) for the original promise because of a feeling that it is not morally fair to demand that someone carry through on a promise to marry, if they stop loving the other person or somehow get 'cold feet', in the meantime.[13] (The more forceful this last consideration seems, the more one will insist that it was wrong to promise on the spur of the moment in the first place.) Moreover, if the woman fails to do what she has promised, it will seem callous or inconsiderate of her to have made that promise; her promise will seem an act of trifling with another human being. But all this hinges utterly, I think, on the assumption that she does, in the end, fail to marry the man, that despite her promise and her compunctions about breaking it, she cannot bring herself to marry him.

For if we suppose that the next day she is upset, perhaps even horrified, at what she has done, but nonetheless, seeing how surprisingly seriously the man takes her promise and how much he depends upon her keeping it, decides to keep her promise (and not hold it against the man), then I think we will be inclined to withdraw the accusation of callousness or trifling. If she in fact marries the man, there will be nothing morally to criticize in her earlier promise; she will have made it (all) right. And this means that both specific and overall moral evaluations of an act done at a particular time may depend on the acts an agent performs subsequently.

Now the idea that the moral character of a later act can depend on what an agent does earlier is familiar and obviously acceptable from the standpoint of ordinary morality. A promise to do something makes a difference to the later rightness or wrongness of not doing that thing. But what I have just suggested is that the sphere of promise-keeping also makes available cases where the rightness of an act seems to depend on what an agent does later. Such examples seem far less recherché than those by which Goldman and Sobel sought to support this notion, and they have an intuitive plausibility in terms of common-sense moral judgments. But before we conclude that we really have found a case where the morality of an act depends on what an agent does later, let me mention briefly one possible objection to the way we have treated the above example. For it might be said that if the woman marries the man, that does not 'make' the earlier act of promising right so much as to make amends for an earlier wrongdoing.

But consider what is typically at stake when an individual's later actions are thought to atone for some earlier wrongdoing: if a man rapes a woman and then, in later contrition, is willing to marry and care for her, perhaps his later actions can make amends for what he did earlier. No one, indeed, would say that the earlier rape had ceased to be a wrongdoing in the light of later actions. Most of us don't think it is all right to rape someone if you (are willing to) marry the victim afterwards, nor do we think it all right to assault someone if you later pay them an amount they would have agreed to in advance as the price for letting you assault them. Permission, we think, is needed in advance and, of course, undoes the accusation of rape.

On the other hand, it does seem reasonable to say that it is morally acceptable (though not, usually, prudent) to promise to marry someone on the spur of the moment if (as long as) you are willing to keep that promise, despite later misgivings. Making such a promise seems wrong only in the light of the expectation that one won't, or probably won't, keep it, whereas a rape or an assault seems wrong quite independently of any expectation that one will or will not marry the girl or pay off the assaulted individual. And that is why it seems implausible to claim that marriage and subsequent good behaviour atone for an earlier impulsive promise to marry in the way marriage and subsequent good behaviour are sometimes thought to atone for an earlier rape. We cannot in this way plausibly avoid the previous conclusion that in the case discussed, and indeed in many others, a person's later actions can help to determine the moral character of his earlier actions.[14]

We see, then, that the idea of covert relationality has application, within the common-sense moral sphere, to certain cases that involve no hint of moral luck. But even though such cases avoid the paradoxical idea of moral luck, they have their own paradoxical character. For in the abstract it seems difficult to believe that an earlier act's moral character could depend (in a way within the agent's control and involving no luck or accident) on what its agent does later. Attributions of overall culpability and of more specific defects like callousness seem to be a matter of what exists at or before the time of the act(s) which ground(s) such attributions, but it is hard to avoid a quite opposite conclusion if one is willing to take seriously the common judgments of (much of) ordinary moral thought with regard to cases like that of the woman who promises marriage. And since an unsuspected dependence on what comes later is common both to the latter case and to certain cases of moral luck (as well as to the non-moral examples we have dealt with), I wonder whether the dependence on what comes later is not perhaps the only paradoxical element in all these cases. In particular, I wonder whether it is any odder to take certain moral-luck-implying cases at face value than any of the other cases we have dealt with; and if it is not, then perhaps the oddness or implausibility of the moral luck involved in such cases in some sense reduces to the oddness or implausibility involved in covert (temporal) relationality. In other words, is the oddness or mystery involved in supposing that a person's culpability (or carelessness) in regard to an act may hinge on subsequent events outside his control anything above and beyond the oddness or mystery involved in supposing that a person's culpability (or callousness) in regard to an act may depend on events later than that act? I am not very sure how to answer that question, but certainly the sheer variety and exuberance of our many examples of (putative) covert relationality might encourage one to think that (to a large extent) the latter phenomenon subsumes and in some degree explains the kind(s) of moral luck we have been talking about.[15]

4

We have focused on cases where a seemingly intrinsic or non-relational property is treated, in common linguistic (and moral) usage, as if it possessed a certain sort of relationality. The relationality has in every case been (partly if not exclusively) temporal: we have uncovered examples of unsuspected dependence on the past or on the future. But those examples are in fact part of a far more general phenomenon. The existence at a given time of a thing of a certain type can surprisingly depend not only what happens earlier or later, but also on what things exist at a *spatial* distance from the thing at the time in question, as the following example should make clear:

Recent advances in medical technology have necessitated a rethinking of the criteria of death. As the means of artificially preserving bodily functions have developed and proliferated, it has been suggested that the functioning of the heart should be replaced, as a criterion of death, by something like irreversible brain-death or irreversible coma. Now without entering into the details of the new forms of technology or into the difficulties of finding a useful, natural, and sufficiently precise criterion or definition of death along these new lines, I want to point out one feature of the new ideas that is particularly relevant to our present discussion. If the death (and presumably, therefore, ceasing to be) of a human being is marked by a state of irreversible coma or brain damage, then what counts as death given present technology may not always count as death, and whether an individual whose body is in a certain sort of internal state counts as dead will (sometimes) depend on surrounding circumstances and in particular on what technology and social relations exist in the world (or immediate environment) in which the deteriorating person finds herself.[16] So if reversibility has a (more or less definitive) role in determining whether someone is alive or dead, we have a case of covert spatial relationality to take a place alongside our earlier examples of covert temporal relationality. It seems unintuitive on the face of it to suppose that the existence of a human being at a given time can depend on coeval factors outside the surface of his body, yet that is precisely what is implied by various recent discussions of the criteria of death.[17]

Now cases of covert temporal and spatial relationality involve us in paradox because they seem to make the existence of a certain sort of individual at a time depend on extrinsic factors. But perhaps the proper response to the vast variety of such cases is, in the end, to question the habits of thought that give rise to the sense of paradox or difficulty. Tyler Burge has recently written of a sort of 'individualism' that understands people and their states of mind solely in terms of what exists or transpires within the boundaries of the individual's body, and he has argued that we should adopt a (somewhat Hegelian) point of view that insists on the role of social institutions in shaping and constituting the individual and the content of his thought.[18] Clearly, the idea that a human being's existence at a time depends only on what is then happening within his body's boundaries, and in no way on coeval surrounding institutions or technology, represents a form of individualism in this sense, and so too presumably does the idea that the existence of a republic at a time cannot hinge on subsequent social and political events. All our cases of covert relationality have, to the extent they stem from plausible independent intuitions, a corrosive effect on individualism in Burge's sense. And in fact Burge himself argues against metaphysical individualism on the basis of *his own* examples of what I have been calling covert relationality. Those examples indicate, to my mind convincingly, that an individual's mental states (e.g., what *de dicto* beliefs he has) can depend in surprising ways on factors outside his body, in particular on his social environment. And to the extent his examples are convincing, we are given further reason to believe covert relationality actually exists, despite the dent that admission makes in some cherished intuitions.[19] Indeed, as we keep getting more and more general in our examples, the option of dismissing the phenomenon of covert relationality as illusory recedes. I have not myself so much offered a thorough account of this phenomenon as given, by examples, some indication of its pervasiveness and tenacity; what we are ultimately to make of covert relationality I am still unclear about, but that we can and should make something significant of it I have almost no doubt at all.

Because of the difficulty of dismissing the whole phenomenon of covert relationality, it is difficult to cast aside the common-sense intuitions that taken collectively point to the possibility of moral luck and of moral act-characterizations that depend on an agent's subsequent actions. And pressure is put on all our (common-sense) intuitions to the contrary. However, Nagel mentions certain forms of moral luck that cannot readily be subsumed under the idea of covert relationality, and this fact may affect the view we ultimately take of any attempt to anchor some kinds of moral luck in the phenomenon of covert relationality. A person's native inclinations and temperament – traits not subject to his own volition or control – are frequently the subject of ordinary moral assessment, and it may also be a matter of accident just what moral tests or moral opportunities a given individual

127

faces. But in neither case does the moral luck involved seem attributable to any form of covert relationality (for detailed discussion of these kinds of luck, see Nagel, *op. cit.*). If one assumes a priori that all classes of moral luck require a uniform explanation (or elimination), then what has been offered above – insofar as the covertly relational cuts across the category of the morally lucky – will automatically seem suspect. But uniform explanations of the whole phenomenon of moral luck seem beyond our reach at the moment and may be impossible in principle. Cases where moral luck concerns the consequences of – or what happens in the spatio-temporal environs of – a given action may differ fundamentally from the sorts of moral luck mentioned just above – it is very hard, at this point, to be sure. And in that case it may be possible to explain both the moral luck of consequences and the dependence of act-assessments on an agent's subsequent actions by relating these (initially) paradoxical common-sense moral notions to the general idea of covert relationality. To the extent that the latter has been made to seem acceptable, we may have succeeded in removing some of the paradox from moral luck and subsequent-action dependence. But given the inconclusiveness of our discussion, I believe common-sense morality continues to face problems from this direction.

CONCLUSION

I would like, by way of conclusion, to draw together some of the separate strings of our discussion in previous chapters and to consider some of the general implications of the approach we have taken to common-sense morality and to consequentialism.

To this end, it might be useful, to begin with, to point out some similarities between what we have been saying here about (various conceptions of) morality and what may, with equal plausibility, be said about (individual) rationality (or reasonableness). We have already seen one such parallel between rationality and morality in our discussion, in Chapter III, of the notion of satisficing. We there saw moral satisficing take its place alongside rational satisficing as a plausible, defensible notion, and just as traditional optimizing (not to mention maximizing) assumptions about rationality are shown to be somewhat limited, or even dubious, by a consideration of the possibility of rational satisficing – whether by individuals or by larger (economic) units, whether in economic contexts or altogether outside the economic sphere – so too, and in much the same way, does the possibility of moral satisficing show the inherent limitations of traditional optimizing and maximizing consequentialism and of similar optimizing assumptions held by common-sense moral theorists. The defensibility of moral satisficing is in part established by (but also partly helps to establish) the defensibility of satisficing as a form of individual (non-moral) rationality.

But other aspects of our discussion also evoke a comparison between morality and rationality, and although we have not yet

129

mentioned these, doing so now will perhaps give further support to some of our earlier conclusions about consequentialist and common-sense morality (moral theory). Thus take, to begin with, what was said in Chapter VI about the possibility of transferring the (consequentialist) moral justification of motives to acts done from those motives. At that time (and relative to an assumed agential or temporal consequentialist perspective) it was claimed that the parent who saves his child rather than a group of others may be acting from a morally good and morally justified motive, but that the act of saving the child may nonetheless count as morally wrong and morally unjustifiable. A similar point was made in connection with the retaliatory mentality: such a mentality may be deterrently useful and morally justifiable even if retaliatory acts done in accordance with that mentality are neither useful nor morally justifiable. And it may somewhat help to ground this sort of moral distinction if we notice that a similar distinction seems to exist in the area of (individual, extramoral) rationality.

Thus consider Newcomb's Problem. Both two-box and one-box solutions to it seem compatible with the admission that, in a universe where individuals were at all likely to be presented with a Newcomb choice, the disposition to pick only one box was a useful and perhaps therefore good disposition for individuals to have. Those with such a disposition will always in Newcomb situations (and given certain simplifying assumptions) end up with a great deal of money; and those with the contrary disposition to pick both boxes will derive very little from Newcomb situations. In such a universe it pays to be a one-boxer, and someone with a one-box disposition has every reason to (try to) retain that disposition, whereas someone with a two-box mentality (may well think he) has reason to turn himself into (what he takes to be) the kind of irrational person who insists on taking only one box.

But what does any of this imply about the rationality of individual actions? The two-box theorist (or any agent disposed to take two boxes) may well grant that a one-box disposition is a more generally useful disposition than his own, but that need not prevent him from contesting the relative usefulness of that disposition *within* some single situation of Newcomb choice. In that situation, he may well argue, the most useful and rational individual act is to take both boxes; what is in the boxes is already fixed, and choosing what is in both of them gives the agent more of what is available in that situation, even if the disposition to make such choices is generally not as useful as the relevant contrary disposition and even if his own possession of such a disposition has given him a less enviable choice in that particular situation than he would have had if he had been differently motivated or had had different views about rationality. So from the standpoint of a two-box Newcomb theorist, at least, there is a distinction to be made between useful general dispositions (which it may be rational to try to cultivate) and what is useful and rational within a particular fixed context of choice, and the possibility of such a distinction may well give some sustenance to the idea of a similar distinction in moral contexts. By the same token, what we have said in Chapter VI about the possibility of distinguishing morally justified motives from morally justified acts done from such motives might possibly itself, in turn, help to support the two-box solution to Newcomb's Problem. However, since the Newcomb Problem involves, and may critically hinge upon, epistemic and other factors that are absent in the case of the parent who saves his own child, it is by no means obvious that our earlier distinctions between the moral justification of motives and the moral justification of actions done from such motives can be used to establish the two-box solution to Newcomb's Problem. And any attempt actually to solve Newcomb's Problem is in any event outside the main focus of the present book, where the emphasis has chiefly been on problems of moral theory. We must be content with noting the similarity between the distinctions drawn in Chapter VI concerning moral justification and those that naturally recommend themselves to two-boxers in discussing the problems of individual rationality that arise out of Newcomb's Problem.

However, the connection between views expressed in the present book about morality and what might be said, along parallel lines, about (individual) rationality is not limited to the two analogies mentioned above. Chapter VII explores the idea of moral luck at some length, but one aspect of the problem of moral luck there left unmentioned is the similarity of that idea to some equally perplexing, but nonetheless equally intuitive things that can be said about the possibility of *rational* luck. It is often thought that one's epistemic or evidential rationality in believing a certain proposition on the basis of certain evidence is a matter solely of how good that evidence is in itself and in relation to one's total evidence and how inherently plausible the believed proposition is by itself (in isolation), but I believe that our common-sense judgments about epistemic (evidential) rationality give the same scope to factors of luck that common-sense moral judgments do, and perhaps the following single example will indicate the sort of thing I have in mind.

Imagine a pair of examiners who have just had the unenviable task of telling a dissertation candidate that his dissertation is unacceptable and requires the most extensive revision of aims and methods in order to stand a chance of acceptance. (Let us not consider how or whether such a dissertation could or should be allowed to get this far.) We may imagine that at the dissertation interview, the examiners were in substantial agreement about the defects of the dissertation, and that the candidate himself, when told of their objections, admitted their force and validity with a rather dejected air of resignation. At the point, however, when the examiners emerge from this meeting, one of them says to the other: I wonder whether he'll appeal the decision to higher university authorities. And the other immediately counters by pointing out that there is no reason for the candidate to appeal, since he himself agreed with the strong and shared objections of both examiners. Hearing this reply, the examiner making the original conjecture about an appeal may well feel that he was being irrational, possibly somewhat paranoid, to suggest the possibility of an appeal. But what happens if out of the blue, a few weeks later, it turns out that the student has gone on to appeal – totally unreasonably, let us assume – the examiners' decision on his dissertation? I think the examiner who originally conjectured that he might do so will tend to revise his view about the irrationality or paranoid quality of his own original conjecture. He will feel, instead, that the course of events has in some measure (perhaps completely) vindicated his original opinion about the real possibility of an appeal.

However, this is a case of rational luck only if we imagine that the conjecturing examiner does not attribute his lack of paranoia, his relative non-irrationality, to some sort of intuitiveness on his part in the original situation where he made his conjecture. If he, or we, imagine that in the original situation he had some clue about the possibility of an appeal from the way the student was

behaving (from the particular or peculiar quality of his deject-
edness, for example), a clue which he received subliminally but
which was nonetheless functioning *as evidence* affecting the
conjectures he was willing to make, then we do not have a case
of rational luck so much as one of subliminal evidence only subsequently recognized as such.

But I don't think there is any need for the conjecturing examiner, or for us, to see his situation, and his subsequent loss of a
sense of being slightly paranoid and irrational, as reflecting the
existence of subliminal evidence and the subsequent recognition
of its presence. The man himself may be led to revise his estim-
ation of his own earlier rationality or irrationality by the mere
fact that his conjecture turned out to be correct. His fears may
seem to be (somewhat) justified *by subsequent events*, rather than
by a subsequently acknowledged earlier bit of evidence, and this
description may indeed be the best expression of the man's own
sense of how he is (turns out to be) justified (or less unjustified
and certainly not paranoid) in his original assumption. Certainly
we ourselves, looking at his situation from the outside, have a
tendency to withhold the judgment of paranoidness and irrationality with regard to his original conjecture in a way we would not
be inclined to do if we imagined instead that no appeal was ever
lodged. If we simply imagine two situations, in one of which his
conjecture turns out correct and in the other of which it does not,
then we will tend to judge him (epistemically) less harshly in the
first situation even without assuming that he must, in that situation, have had available and been subliminally following clues
provided by the candidate himself (or by other known facts about
the candidate). Even imagining that the candidate provided no
such clues, our judgment as to (degree of) irrationality and
paranoidness can be, and in common-sense terms usually is,
affected by how we imagine things actually turning out, and this
provides for a possibility of (epistemic) rational luck that is quite
similar to what we said in Chapter VII about the common-sense
possibilities of moral luck.

So there are a number of parallels to be drawn between rationality and morality in connection with some of the major themes
of the present book. But the book's discussion of the nature and
interrelations of common-sense morality and consequentialism
also has a certain direction that it is at this point worth trying to

say something about. And since our focus on common-sense morality and consequentialism is more than slightly reminiscent of Sidgwick's great book, I think the general thrust of the present book's argument is perhaps best understood and summarized in terms of a brief comparison with the aims and arguments of *The Methods of Ethics*.

Sidgwick's discussion of common-sense morality and utilitarianism aims to be far more systematic and comprehensive than anything attempted here. But by his own admission, he does not seek to prove or establish any one moral 'method' over all others. Although he clearly shows a preference for utilitarianism over ethical egoism and common-sense morality and attempts both to emend and justify the main body of common-sense morality in utilitarian moral-theoretic terms, he also expresses serious doubts about the rationality or justifiability of the utilitarian method and his book ends on a somewhat sceptical note. Nevertheless, Sidgwick does evince both a preference and a hope in favour of utilitarianism, and to that extent the tendencies and conclusions of the present book are perhaps both more neutral and less hopeful than those of *The Methods of Ethics*. The process of comparing common-sense morality and consequentialism and of investigating tendencies that seem inherent in these moral positions taken separately has led us, through the course of previous chapters, to a point where both consequentialism and common-sense morality seem more perplexing, more problematic, than they may previously have seemed to be; but this process of attrition, both external and internal, does not appear to favour either of these moral positions over the other.

Thus when we recognize the existence of the self-other asymmetry of common-sense morality, that asymmetry can be made to appear puzzling not only from a consequentialist standpoint but in the light of the difficulty of understanding or justifying such an asymmetry even in terms acceptable to common-sense morality. On the other hand, some of the oddness and difficulty of common-sense morality's admissions of moral luck stem not so much from any divergence here from consequentialism, as from the very fact that common-sense morality, having denied, in its deontological 'part', that acts should be entirely ruled by consequences, seems in another of its 'parts' to place an unreasonable and unjustifiable emphasis precisely *on* consequences.

By the same token, we saw that although some criticisms of consequentialism (e.g., the argument from moral autonomy against the consequentialist view of individual moral obligation) arise out of common-sense morality and gain sustenance from the strong intuitions lying behind the latter, some of the most forceful criticisms of consequentialism arise from within consequentialism itself. Consequentialism allows for satisficing versions of itself and can thus be criticized for an unreasonable (practically) exclusive preoccupation with optimizing and maximizing forms of consequentialist moral theory. But then the very possibility of non-optimizing forms of consequentialism leads naturally to the idea that both optimizing and satisficing forms of consequentialism may well be more arbitrary than the sort of scalar consequentialism developed in Chapter V, and the discussion then redounds to the disfavour of the non-scalar common-sense morality of benevolence as well. (The way to these further moves is smoothed, of course, by the discussion, in Chapter IV, of the non-practical character both of the principle of utility and of certain important parts of the common-sense morality of actions.) Chapter VI then goes on to argue that the divorce consequentialism allows between the valid standard(s) of morality and the practical regulation of action, taken together with the preference it gives to an impersonal detached standpoint as the fulcrum of moral judgment and justification, leads, or seems to lead, naturally to the dissolution of consequentialism as a moral theory (about consequences).

To all this extent, the tendency of the present book has been critical, has been to point up aspects of common-sense morality and consequentialism that make difficulties for each of these theories. Even though I am no sceptic about morality, I think these difficulties must be faced before we can evaluate the relative merits of consequentialism and common-sense morality or find some other theoretical moral position superior to either of them.

When I began to think about the problems discussed in the preceding chapters, I hoped to be able to defend common-sense morality against consequentialism (unlike Sidgwick, I wanted to focus on consequentialism generally, rather than attempting to justify or pinpoint the specific difficulties of one particular variety of consequentialism, utilitarianism). In the course of writing this book (especially in the light of Chapter I), I came to think that consequentialism was perhaps in better shape (relative to common-sense morality) than I had realized. I also believe that satisficing consequentialism offers the consequentialist some opportunities for interesting development and, in addition, for doing something to square his view with strong common-sense intuitions about the moral autonomy of individuals. And in that connection, I offered a brief underlying account of the moral psychology of moral and rational satisficing that may do something to make the idea of moral satisficing seem (more) acceptable to consequentialists.

Sidgwick, of course, provided, and laid great emphasis on providing, moral-psychological (and metaphysical) underpinnings for his defence (to the extent it was a defence) of utilitarianism, and this aspect of Sidgwick's work has been an inspiration to philosophers of many different persuasions. But by comparison with what is attempted in Chapter III, the attempt in Chapters V and VI to push beyond the satisficing/optimizing distinction and then to question the opposition of agent-factors to all sorts of factors that underlie good total sequences of events was somewhat lacking in (realistic, as opposed to hypothetical) moral-psychological underpinnings. The argument of these latter chapters proceeds largely by reference to purely metaphysical considerations, and that very fact, the absence of anything suitably realistic, moral-psychologically, in the motivation of their argument, may well make one dubious about the conclusions of those chapters in a way that we have, I think, no reason to be dubious about the method and argument of Chapter III taken by themselves. I somehow hope, then, that some reason can be found to stop the arguments in Chapters V and VI and thereby persuade us (in our consequentialist moods at least) to rest content with some form of satisficing consequentialism.

On the other hand, it would also be helpful – since most of us are likely to continue to think in common-sense moral terms most of the time – if we could find some way of understanding and even justifying deontological side-constraints, the self-other asymmetry, and the idea of moral luck. Some preliminary things were said in favour of common-sense moral ideas in Chapters I, II and VII, but obviously a great deal of work remains to be done if one wants to proceed confidently and conscientiously in that direction. On the other hand, common-sense morality and consequentialism are not the only alternatives in moral theory; and given our heightened sense of their difficulties, we may well have reason at this point to turn (again) to Kantian moral theory and its Rawlsian variant or – in the light of the failure of practicality at the heart of common-sense and consequentialist morality – to theories, of the sort prevalent in Greek ethics, that focus on excellence of character rather than acts, but judge such excellence in non-consequentialist terms.

NOTES

CHAPTER I COMMON-SENSE MORALITY AND CONSEQUENTIALISM

[1] Any moral theory that makes right and wrong action depend entirely on results or consequences is act-consequentialist. A theory holding that an act is right if and only if it produces the best state(s) of affairs may go on to claim that certain considerations of justice are relevant to the goodness of overall states of affairs. Such a theory will be act-consequentialist but not act-utilitarian. Cf. Amartya Sen, 'Utilitarianism and Welfarism', *Journal of Philosophy*, 76, 1979, pp. 463–89; and Samuel Scheffler, *The Rejection of Consequentialism*, Oxford University Press, 1982, ch. 2 and pp. 72ff.

[2] I shall not be discussing those cases where desire for the optimal course of events may lead one to qualify act-consequentialism into some form of act-and-motive consequentialism. (Cf. R. M. Adams, 'Motive Utilitarianism', *Journal of Philosophy*, 73, 1976, pp. 467–81.) Because other forms of consequentialism are not immediately relevant to the main conclusions of the present chapter, I shall for the moment drop the word 'act' in speaking of act-utilitarianism and act-consequentialism. Note too that the connection between benevolence and optimality assumed in the main text will be called into question in Chapter III, below.

[3] See Williams's 'A Critique of Utilitarianism' in Smart and Williams, *Utilitarianism: For and Against*, Cambridge, 1973; T. Nagel's 'The Limits of Objectivity', in S. McMurrin, ed., *The Tanner Lectures on Human Value*, I, Cambridge University Press, 1980, pp. 119ff.; and S. Scheffler, *op. cit.*, *passim*. Nagel also discusses some of the reasons why the impersonal standpoint itself is so appealing in ethics and elsewhere.

[4] See W. D. Ross, *The Foundations of Ethics*, Oxford University Press,

1939, pp. 72ff., 272ff. Cf. Sidgwick, *The Methods of Ethics*, London, Macmillan, 1962, 7th edn., pp. 431f.

5 One can imagine either that one kills oneself, knowing that the organs will be thus used, or that with superior technology and equipment one actually brings about the requisite operation on oneself.

6 E.g., by Robert Nozick in *Anarchy, State, and Utopia*, New York, Basic Books, 1974, p. 30; by Thomas Nagel, *op. cit.*; and by S. Scheffler, *op. cit.*, esp. ch. 4 and p. 121. I am especially indebted to Scheffler's formulation of these particular problems.

7 Interestingly, Scheffler never remarks on the self-other asymmetry of ordinary deontological restrictions and in fact always formulates those restrictions in *symmetric* form. He says, e.g., that they are restrictions against 'harming some undeserving person'. I have found only one place where the asymmetry slips in unnoticed (p. 100).

8 In deprecating oneself, one may 'do oneself an injustice', but this is presumably not the morally relevant sense of the notion.

9 On the other hand, a kind of moral-theoretic methodological conservatism may indicate that we not abandon common-sense morality until we are given strong reasons to do so.

10 The distinction, roughly, is between an asymmetry concerning omissions and one concerning commissions. But Nagel (*op. cit.*) has argued that deontological restrictions concern even what one intentionally *allows*. According to Nagel, roughly, one may not deliberately allow someone to die as a means to prevent other deaths (or to prevent other people intentionally allowing people to die). I have stated the asymmetry regarding the allocation of harms and benefits so that it lies outside even this broad, intentional-omission-including notion of deontological constraints, by speaking of the difference between ignoring benefits (harms) to oneself and to others – where such ignoring may not involve intentionally or deliberately failing to prevent harms or benefits, but simply *not bothering* about them. The self-other asymmetry is thus not entirely limited to the usual area of side-constraints or deontological restrictions.

11 However, consider the qualification mentioned in note 2, above.

12 On this point see, e.g., Sidgwick, *op. cit.*, p. 246.

13 See, e.g. Nozick, *op. cit.*, p. 30n.; for some problems about defining the morally relevant sense of 'innocent', also see Nozick, *op. cit.*

14 See J. Thomson, 'Killing, Letting Die, and the Trolley Problem', *The Monist*, 59, 1976, pp. 204–17.

15 Arguments of both these sorts can be found in Jonathan Bennett's 'Morality and Consequences', in S. McMurrin, ed., *The Tanner Lectures on Human Values*, II, Cambridge University Press, 1981, pp. 45–116.

16 See his 'Doing Good: the Right and the Wrong Way', *Journal of Philosophy*, 79, 1982, pp. 439–55.

17 See Scheffler, *op. cit.*

18 See Bernard Williams, *op. cit.*, section 5.

19 See Scheffler, *op. cit.*

20 Don't say: 'but the consent in the first case is of another person and one should not take another person's consent as seriously (as literally) as one takes one's own.' That is just our asymmetry in another guise. Also, I have ruled out of consideration any religious injunctions against suicide that might make the cases seem more similar. Perhaps, I should say that the asymmetry I am speaking of is one of common-sense *secular* morality.

21 In *The Object of Morality*, London, Methuen, 1976, p. 26.

22 By the same token, sociobiological explanations of ordinary morality that focus on the evolutionary effects of altruism seem also to be incapable of motivating or accounting for the self-other asymmetry. If the gene-survival value of altruism explains the existence of moral imperatives concerning others, why shouldn't the survival value of self-concern have generated similar imperatives concerning one's behaviour towards oneself?

CHAPTER II MORAL AUTONOMY

1 The *obligation* not to kill one individual even as a means to saving five different individuals entails, except, possibly, under certain conditions of moral conflict, a *permission* not to kill one to save five. But in speaking above and elsewhere of (the whole class of) common-sense moral permissions I mean to exclude such obligation-based permissions and to be speaking of what are more naturally thought of as permissions, namely, permissions not tied to specific obligations, where what one is permitted to do one is also permitted not to do.

2 It would be a mistake to object that if the actually selfish agent were to sacrifice his own well-being, then such self-sacrifice would be among his projects and justifiable accordingly. For one thing, the counterfactual claim involved here cannot be sustained. We can say that he would make the sacrifice only if he were unselfish, but not that if he made the sacrifice, he would be unselfish. Cf. 'Time in Counterfactuals', *Philosophical Review*, 87, 1978, pp. 3–27.

3 See especially his 'A Critique of Utilitarianism' in Smart and Williams, *Utilitarianism: For and Against*, Cambridge University Press, 1973, section 5.

4 See, for example, Scheffler, *The Rejection of Consequentialism*, Oxford, 1982, esp. pp. 20, 25, 125. Also my own previous 'The Morality of Wealth', in Aiken and La Follette, eds, *World Hunger and Moral Obligation*, Englewood Cliffs, N. J., Prentice-Hall, 1977, esp. pp. 125f., which makes, in addition, an appeal to something like Williams's notion of integrity. Obviously the claim that a moral principle unreasonably interferes with the moral individual's deepest identity, or integrity, is akin to the claim that it demands too much in the way of sacrifice (is objectionably demanding).

5 The qualification 'innocent' is essential if we wish to express the

common-sense moral view of our permissions to pursue projects or commitments. One's project cannot permissibly be genocide or success in the Mafia. On this compare Scheffler, *op. cit.*, p. 18; and 'The Morality of Wealth', pp. 126ff. The notion of innocence needs further specification, but can, I think, serve our present purposes undefined.

6 It may in some sense be psychologically impossible for a certain individual to become interested in the history of philosophy, but this needn't interfere with our judgment that a career in that area is morally permissible to him, any more than the fact that a certain individual is irredeemably selfish prevents him from being permitted to act unselfishly on a given occasion.

7 See 'Ifs and Cans' in *Philosophical Papers*, Oxford, Clarendon, 1961, pp. 157ff.

8 Austin, in passing, gives some examples of ordinary language quantifications implicitly involving non-conditional 'ifs', but never explicitly draws our attention to this fact about them. The examples are, in fact, closely related to those discussed here.

9 The permission to pursue any project one wants is not, therefore, like an injunction to pay off one's long-standing debts, which makes the obligation (need) to pay off a debt conditional upon the debt's being long-standing. Rather, it is like an unconditionally licensing 'do whatever you want', which is not to be understood as the merely conditional 'do whatever in fact accords with your actual wants'.

10 Together with the suggestion or implication that it is unclear which project one will actually choose. See Austin, *op. cit.*

11 Certain related strands in the ordinary notion of autonomy and philosophical definitions of autonomy are not immediately relevant to present purposes and will not be discussed here.

12 Thomas Nagel invokes the term 'autonomy' in discussing the permissions (reasons) agents have to devote themselves to their own valued projects and commitments. (See his 'The Limits of Objectivity' in S. McMurrin, ed., *The Tanner Lectures on Human Values*, I, University of Utah Press and Cambridge University Press, 1980, pp. 119ff.) However, like others who have recently discussed the limitations of act-utilitarian morality, he ignores permissions connected with projects (and commitments) that an agent is not actually interested in and focuses on the justification one has for pursuing projects one is actually committed to. So he conceives autonomy in a much narrower fashion than common usage makes possible, though the term is certainly not a misnomer for what he has in mind.

However, Nagel also seeks to vindicate the agent's fulfilment of his *desires*, not merely of his *projects* and *commitments*, and thus indirectly raises the question whether our moral autonomy extends to the fulfilment of desires totally unconnected with anything as serious as a life project or personal commitment. To take an extreme example, is the (ideal-typic) South Sea Islander morally permitted to lead a carefree existence or does he act wrongly through a lack of personal and moral seriousness? (Or does his childlike lack of seriousness disqualify him as a moral agent?) I am not sure how to answer these questions or thus whether the notion of moral autonomy should be extended in this direction, but an exclusive emphasis on projects and commitments conveys the unfortunate suggestion – consider the similar implausibilities to which utilitarianism is driven – that moral permission to eat a good meal derives directly or indirectly from one's permission to pursue some serious project or commitment and/or from certain duties. It also suggests, again unfortunately, that one may be morally permitted to pursue the project of becoming as much as possible like a carefree, projectless South Sea Islander, even if the Islander herself has no permission to be and act as she does.

13 Scheffler's chief defence of permissions to pursue one's own projects and commitments refers not to the objectionable demandingness of the act-utilitarian principle, but to the fact that such projects and commitments are generated and pursued independently of the impersonal standpoint that gives utilitarianism so much of its appeal. But it is not clear whether the 'natural independence of the personal point of view' provides a rationale for our permission to pursue any innocent project whatever or merely for our permission to pursue those personal projects in which interest actually is generated and sustained. Scheffler himself attempts to justify only the latter.

14 It is tempting to think that the idea of autonomy can account for our permission to hurt or kill ourselves in order to prevent greater harm to others and thereby somehow also account for the self-other asymmetry of deontological side-constraints, but the temptation must be resisted. Appeals merely to autonomy can end up justifying too much, and the problem remains why an appeal to agent-autonomy can perhaps reasonably justify hurting oneself in order to help others but cannot (at least for common moral thinking) justify one in hurting people other than oneself in order to prevent a (greater) number of quite different people from being hurt.

CHAPTER III SATISFICING CONSEQUENTIALISM

1 It would seem that consequentialism need not be committed to the possibility of ranking all possible states of affairs, but only to the possibility of ranking possible outcomes or consequences of actions, i.e., states of affairs that appropriately include the doing of some (possible, available) act. Also, some recent discussions suggest reasons why sequences of acts rather than single acts should be the subject of consequentialist assessment, but I shall for the most part ignore this issue. The discussion that follows should explain how a satisficing form of act-sequence-consequentialism could be defended. (On the evaluation of sequences, see, for example, Holly Goldman, 'Doing the Best One Can', in A. Goldman and J. Kim, eds, *Values and*

Morals, Dordrecht, Reidel, 1978, pp. 185–214.)

2 This characterization ignores various forms of average utilitarianism. For a technically more precise elaboration of some of these distinctions, see A. K. Sen, 'Utilitarianism and Welfarism', *Journal of Philosophy*, 76, 1979, pp. 463ff.

3 Surely, it would be terminologically odd to treat someone who affirmed what I am going to call 'satisficing consequentialism' as *denying* consequentialism, yet this is precisely what present-day terminology requires – see, for example, Bernard Williams, 'A Critique of Utilitarianism', in Smart and Williams, *Utilitarianism: For and Against*, Cambridge University Press, 1973, p. 90.

Incidentally, the possibility of satisficing (act-consequentialism is (I believe) unintentionally suggested by things said in the Introduction to Sen and Williams, eds, *Utilitarianism and Beyond* (Cambridge University Press, 1982, pp. 3f.). At one point, consequentialism is simply characterized as a theory 'which claims that actions are to be chosen on the basis of the states of affairs which are their consequences. . .' and this is neutral as between optimizing and satisficing forms of consequentialism. However, the Introduction goes on to treat consequentialism as involving the production of optimal consequences and the possibility of consequentialist moral satsificing is never mentioned. Certainly, in Sen, *op. cit.*, consequentialism is *defined* in terms of optimal consequences.

4 See, e.g., Rawls, *A Theory of Justice*, Cambridge, Mass., Harvard University Press, 1971, pp. 23ff., 416ff.

5 For relevant discussions in the economics literature of satisficing, see, e.g., H. Simon, 'A Behavioral Model of Rational Choice', *Quarterly Journal of Economics*, 69, 1955, pp. 99–118; Simon, 'Theories of Decision Making in Economics and Behavioral Science', *American Economic Review*, 49, 1959, pp. 253–83; Simon, *Administrative Behavior*, N.Y., Macmillan, 1961, 2nd edn; and R. Cyert and J. March, eds, *A Behavioral Theory of the Firm*, Englewood Cliffs, N.J., Prentice-Hall, 1963.

6 A person whose desires are moderate or modest might also be called 'temperate', but what we have been saying about the habit of moderation is very different from what Aristotle says about what he calls the virtue of temperance. On Aristotle's conception a temperate individual has the right amount of desire for the right sorts of things, etc., and such rightness, roughly, involves a mean between two less right extremes. But our talk of moderation in the text above is not supposed to imply that taking more than moderation would allow is in any way wrong or unreasonable. Moderation involves a mean between extremes that are not necessarily (both) more undesirable than moderation itself is. And it is possible to use the notion of 'temperance' or 'temperateness' in a similarly non-Aristotelian and (relatively) value-free way.

7 Is modesty or moderation, then, a form of puritanism? Not if puritanism involves asceticism, but, on the other hand, it may be favoured

by certain forms of puritanism. Surely that fact alone can hardly make it suspect. Incidentally, *rational* satisficing seems to involve not only a disinclination to optimize, but a reasonable sense of when one has enough. To be content with much less than one should be is (can be) one form of *bathos*.

8 See Simon, 'Decision Making in Economics and Behavioral Science'.

9 It may always be possible to devise an artificial function according to which satisficing behaviour would automatically be interpretable as maximizing (or optimizing), but those who have assumed that all rational action involves maximization would presumably not wish to rely on such an artificial defence of that thesis. Their idea, rather, has been that even when behaviour appears not to involve any form of maximizing, there are always hidden or underlying factors in the light of which that behaviour is in the most natural sense considered maximizing. But this a priori conviction must surely be weakened by the phenomenological naturalness and sheer number of cases in which human beings appear to satisfice – as well as by the satisficing models of behaviour that have been developed within the recent literature of economics. (Compare what has been said for and against psychological egoism.)

10 Nor, judging by the tales themselves, do we have any reason to suppose that wishers ask for less than they could in order to please (not offend) the wish grantor or in order not to be corrupted by having too much wealth.

Note further that the choice of modest well-being (wealth) cannot simply be faulted on the grounds that the chooser has no reason to prefer it to some higher level of well-being (and wealth). In the first place, it is not a general condition of rationality that in choosing between two options one has reason to choose one of those options rather than the other: where, e.g., two equally good options present themselves, it need not be irrational to choose one of them, even though one has no reason to prefer it to the other. In the second place, reasons can be relative to an individual's concerns, his world view, or even his habits; and from the distinctive standpoint of the moderate individual, there may well be a reason to prefer moderate wealth (well-being) to great wealth. The fact that great wealth is much more than he needs (or cares about) can count, for such an individual, as a reason for not choosing great wealth (but not as a reason for refusing modest wealth). I am indebted here to criticisms made by Philip Pettit in his contribution to the symposium on 'Satisficing Consequentialism' in the *Proceedings of the Aristotelian Society*, supplementary volume, 1984. (The present chapter is an expanded version of my own contribution to the same symposium.)

11 For a rather similar point about the way a virtuous individual thinks about personal goods that can only be unjustly obtained, see my *Goods and Virtues*, Oxford, 1983, ch. 5.

12 In fact, it is hard to see how any specific monetary wish can be optimizing if the individual is unsure about his own marginal utility

curve for the use of money (and not worried about being corrupted, becoming blasé, etc.). To that extent, we are all *necessarily* satisficers in situations where we can wish for whatever we want, unless, perhaps, we are allowed to wish for our own greatest future well-being in those very terms. If satisficing were irrational, would that mean that anything other than such an explicitly optimizing wish would be irrational?

13 See *The Open Society and its Enemies*, London, Routledge & Kegan Paul, 1974, vol. I, ch. 5, note 6; chapter 9, note 2.

14 For another discussion of our common-sense satisficing moral intuitions, see R. M. Adams, 'Must God Create the Best?', *Philosophical Review*, 81, 1972, pp. 317–32.

15 The point is made by R. N. Smart in 'Negative Utilitarianism', *Mind*, 67, 1958, pp. 542f.

16 See the J. H. Burns and H. L. A. Hart edition of Bentham's *Introduction*, London, Methuen, 1982, pp. 11f. However, also see p. 282.

17 Recent moral philosophy has taken very seriously the possibility that an agent might through no fault of his own be put in a situation of moral tragedy where he cannot avoid acting wrongly. But surely there are cases where anything one does will have bad consequences (in the permissive utilitarian sense of the term), yet where it is not wrong to perform an act with fewer bad consequences than any feasible alternative.

18 The point is made by Scheffler, *The Rejection of Consequentialism*, Oxford, 1982; also in my previous 'The Morality of Wealth', in Aiken and LaFollette, eds, *World Hunger and Moral Obligation*, Englewood Cliffs, N.J., Prentice-Hall, 1977, pp. 124–47.

19 In 'Evaluator Relativity and Consequentialist Evaluation' (*Philosophy and Public Affairs*, 12, 1983, pp. 113–32), Amartya Sen has recently suggested (roughly) that an act's rightness may depend on whether it produces consequences that are best-from-the-standpoint-of-the-agent. Such a theory, despite the lack of historical antecedents, is arguably act-consequentialist and would permit the pursuit of individual projects. Unfortunately, it also seems to make such pursuit obligatory – perhaps this could be avoided by adopting a satisficing version of the theory.

20 Bentham, *op. cit.*, p. 100.

21 Sidgwick, *Methods of Ethics*, London, Macmillan, 1962, 7th edn, p. 428.

22 R. M. Adams, 'Motive Utilitarianism', *Journal of Philosophy*, 76, 1979, pp. 467–81.

23 Cf. Sidgwick, *op. cit.*, p. 428; Adams, 'Motive Utilitarianism'; and R. M. Hare, *Moral Thinking*, Oxford University Press, 1982. In Chapter VI we shall be considering at some length whether a consequentialist morality of motives really can serve to justify – in consequentialist moral terms – certain acts that are wrong by some act-consequentialist standard.

24 See Sidgwick, *op. cit.*, e.g., pp. 285–89; also p. 95. The confusion can also be found in Mill's 'Utilitarianism'.

CHAPTER IV MORALITY AND THE PRACTICAL

1 P. R. Foot, 'Morality as a System of Hypothetical Imperatives', *Philosophical Review*, 81, 1972, pp. 305–16. Cf. Jan Narveson's claim (in *Morality and Utility*, Baltimore, Johns Hopkins, 1967, p. 105) that a principle doesn't count as ethical unless it is action-guiding.

2 See, for example, Kant's *Critique of Practical Reason*, pt 1, bk 1, ch. 1, section 1.

3 Cf. Foot, *op. cit.*, pp. 305–7.

4 S. N. Hampshire, 'Fallacies in Moral Philosophy', *Mind*, 58, 1949, pp. 466–82.

5 See Sidgwick's *The Methods of Ethics*, London, Macmillan, 1962, 7th edn, pp. 413, 469, 480–92; R. E. Bales, 'Act-Utilitarianism: Account of Right-Making Characteristics or Decision-Making Procedure?', *American Philosophical Quarterly*, 8, 1971, pp. 257–65; and S. Scheffler, *The Rejection of Consequentialism*, Oxford University Press, 1982, ch. 3.

6 Such a view is implicit in Bernard Williams, 'A Critique of Utilitarianism', in Smart and Williams, *Utilitarianism: For and Against*, Cambridge University Press, 1973, pp. 121–35; and in Michael Stocker, 'The Schizophrenia of Modern Ethical Theories', *Journal of Philosophy*, 73, 1976, pp. 453–66.

7 I do not think recourse to the unconscious will help the traditional view at this point. Even if one who kills in self-defence is unconsciously aware that what he is doing is morally justified, it is hard to believe that that belief/knowledge will affect the mainsprings of self-protective action or exert a major influence on what the self-defender does.

8 However, none of the above should be taken to imply that our sense of what is *necessary* to our own self-defence cannot evolve in response to experience and acquired knowledge.

9 In P. Foot, 'Are Moral Considerations Overriding?' in *Virtues and Vices*, Oxford, Basil Blackwell, 1978, pp. 186f.

10 I take it that rules, precepts, prescriptions, 'imperatives', and injunctions are all practical by definition. But principles exist in metaphysics and pure mathematics and are not practical *ex vi terminorum*.

11 In *Freedom and Reason*, Oxford, 1965, pp. 196ff., Hare makes it quite clear that he regards all principles of permission as prescriptive and practical.

12 Foot in 'Virtues and Vices', *Virtues and Vices*, pp. 13f.; Stocker in 'The Schizophrenia of Modern Ethical Theories', esp. pp. 462f.

13 On the other hand, a duty to visit sick friends *from sympathy* would involve a failure of practicality right at the heart of morality. But it is implausible to suppose such a duty exists, partly for reasons just mentioned and in part because most of us think morality cannot properly 'legislate for feeling'.

14 In B. Williams, *Moral Luck*, Cambridge University Press, 1981.

15 E.g., J. J. C. Smart in 'An Outline of a System of Utilitarian Ethics'

in Smart and Williams, *op. cit.*, pp. 44ff. On the reasons against inculcating or practising act-utilitarianism, see, e.g., Sidgwick, *loc. cit.*

16 One cannot render the utilitarian principle completely practical by altering it to read: one has an obligation to seek the maximization of utility unless spontaneity would achieve better results. For the latter incoherently assumes that spontaneity can be governed by a principle recommending spontaneity.

17 See Stocker, *op. cit.*; and B. A. O. Williams, 'A Critique of Utilitarianism', in Smart and Williams, *op. cit.*, pp. 121ff.

18 Other forms of (utilitarian) consequentialism are based on principles of act-appraisal that cannot be regarded as practical. The principle (mentioned but left nameless by Williams, 'A Critique . . .', p. 121) that an act is right if it expresses a utilitarianly valuable character-disposition is clearly not for the guidance of action, since we cannot sensibly ask someone to *act from* a maximizing character-disposition. (But is this principle plausible? Williams doesn't appear to think so.) By contrast, typical rule-utilitarianism and the 'conscience-utilitarianism' offered recently by Robert M. Adams (in 'Motive Utilitarianism', *Journal of Philosophy*, 73, 1976, p. 479) do have a practical character: it makes sense to ask someone to do the things that would be demanded by a maximizing set of rules or conscience.

In the article cited, however, Adams also discusses the motive utilitarian view that (roughly) motives are right or good to the extent that they serve utility. This principle may or may not be plausible, but in any event it is clearly not practical (as Adams himself seems well aware). However, the principle concerns the evaluation of motives, not of actions, and many of us already believe that principles for the moral appraisal of motives (or character) need not be practical. What is distinctive about the examples discussed here, on the other hand, is their tendency to show that certain common-sense standards for morally appraising actions cannot reasonably be addressed to moral agents.

19 Cf. John Elster, *Ulysses and the Sirens*, Cambridge University Press, 1979, p. 168. Also Williams, *op. cit.*, pp. 128ff.

CHAPTER V SCALAR MORALITY

1 See Adams, 'Motive Utilitarianism', *Journal of Philosophy*, 73, 1976, p. 470; and Sidgwick, *Methods of Ethics*, London, Macmillan, 1962, p. 413.

2 Actually, I mentioned one possible such reason in Chapter III, when I spoke of the desire, on the part of some consequentialists, to provide moral justification for certain sorts of wrong actions by citing the goodness of the motive behind such actions. It is easier to do this if the standard for goodness in motives is a satisficing, rather than optimizing one; but in Chapter VI it will be argued that the consequentialist

cannot justify immoral actions in this way; and in that case the above-mentioned reason for preferring satisficing motive-consequentialism is undercut.

3 With regard to situations where one can do (more or less) good on balance, such a theory might make only the safe positive judgments that doing no good (on balance) is wrong and doing the most good possible (on balance) is right. Cases where one cannot on balance achieve any good require a more complicated treatment, but there is no need to discuss the complications here. Also, I shall not attempt to decide whether a scalar morality of actions should concern itself with the comparison of *non-alternative* actions facing different agents or the same agent at different times.

4 For discussion of our obligations to those we have wronged see, e.g., Robert Nozick's *Anarchy, State, and Utopia*, New York, Basic Books, 1974.

5 On this point, see, for example, Peter Singer's 'Famine, Affluence, and Morality', in W. Aiken and H. LaFollette, eds, *World Hunger and Moral Obligation*, Englewood Cliffs, N.J., Prentice-Hall, 1977, p. 24. One dissenter is Bernard Gert in *The Moral Rules*, New York, Harper & Row, 1966, p. 73; but the reasons he gives for denying that we ever have an obligation to help others in distress (whom we have not harmed) seem very flimsy.

6 I advocated such a principle in 'The Morality of Wealth', in Aiken and LaFollette, eds, *op. cit.*, pp. 124ff.; the moral importance of (life) projects or plans is, of course, emphasized by Bernard Williams in 'A Critique of Utilitarianism', in Smart and Williams, *Utilitarianism: For and Against*, Cambridge University Press, 1973, section 5. In *A Theory of Justice* (Cambridge, Mass., Harvard University Press, 1971, pp. 114, 117), Rawls's view of our obligations of benevolence seems to drift or range between the requirement of sporadic, occasional charity and the stronger demand that we give as much as we can give without disrupting our life plans.

7 See Singer, *op. cit.*

8 Except, perhaps, for such common-sense positive judgments as that one ought (is wrong not) to help others when one can do so without *excessive* risk or loss to oneself, or without making *too much* of a sacrifice. (Cf. Rawls, *op. cit.*) But I don't think such principles are helpful enough (informative enough) to dissuade us from shifting over to a scalar morality of benevolence.

9 As I mentioned in the previous chapter, Bernard Williams and Michael Stocker both seem to argue in this direction.

10 There is also the possibility that a moral agent may be, or take himself to be, justified (overall) in doing what he regards as morally wrong; and here again, moral wrongness is not, even for a moral agent, an absolute guide concerning what to do. I have discussed the possibility of such cases in *Goods and Virtues*, Oxford University Press, 1983, ch. 4; and we shall be considering them again, at some length, in Chapter VI, below.

11 In *Practical Ethics* (Cambridge University Press, 1979, pp. 180f.),
  Peter Singer suggests that adhering to a principle of tithing might well
  produce better results (in terms of benevolence) than adherence to the
  more demanding principle of benevolence (mentioned in the text
  above) that he believes is actually correct. The idea that more
  demanding principles may produce less good results is also considered
  in 'The Morality of Wealth', pp. 130ff.

12 See, for example, G. E. M. Anscombe's 'Modern Moral Philosophy',
  Philosophy, 33, 1958, pp. 1–19.

13 In this connection, compare some of the things Robert Nozick (*op.
  cit.*, p. 30n.) and Samuel Scheffler (*The Rejection of Consequentialism*,
  Oxford University Press, 1982, pp. 39, 85f.) say about the ways in
  which deontological restrictions may (might) be overridden in the
  name of consequences – and contrast with Anscombe, *op. cit.* In
  the text above, I have also ignored the possibility that when and if
  considerations of catastrophic or (relatively) dire consequences override deontological restrictions, they do so not in the name of morality,
  but in the name of some (non-egocentric) good that *justifies* one in
  overriding the restrictions but does not make it *morally right* to do so.
  Perhaps, in other words, the deontological side-constraints against,
  e.g., certain (possibly highly qualified) sorts of killing really are absolute moral side-constraints, and our feeling that we may sometimes be
  justified in contravening them should be taken as evidence for the
  possibility of justified (even admirable) immorality. I have argued for
  such an interpretation of the violation of certain side-constraints in
  Goods and Virtues, pp. 97ff., but in many cases it seems possible that
  the violation of some common-sense restriction is *morally* justifiable
  in terms of consequences (the averting of catastrophe, for example),
  and it is the latter possibility that suggests the idea of a scalar deontology of restrictions against killing and the like.

CHAPTER VI CONSEQUENTIALISM AND BEYOND

1 See, e.g., Sidgwick's *The Methods of Ethics*, London, Macmillan,
  1962, 7th edn, p. 428.

2 This particular form of argument appears in Derek Parfit's *Reasons
  and Persons*, Oxford University Press, 1984, Part One.

3 *Goods and Virtues*, Oxford University Press, 1983, ch. 4.

4 The idea that such behaviour is automatically unfree is very effectively
  scotched in R. M. Adams's 'Motive Utilitarianism', *Journal of Philosophy*, 73, 1976, p. 473. For further development, see my 'Selective
  Necessity and the Free-will Problem', *Journal of Philosophy*, 79, 1982,
  pp. 5–24.

5 In 'Persons, Character, and Morality', reprinted in *Moral Luck*,
  Cambridge University Press, 1981.

6 On this point see Samuel Scheffler's *The Rejection of Consequen-*

tialism, Oxford University Press, 1982, pp. 2, 123ff.; Thomas Nagel, 'Subjective and Objective', in *Mortal Questions*, Cambridge, 1979, pp. 202ff.; and Nagel, 'The Limits of Objectivity', in S. McMurrin, ed., *The Tanner Lectures on Human Values* I, University of Utah and Cambridge University Press, 1980, pp. 117–39.

Incidentally, the difference between the most fundamental consequentialist moral motivation and the fundamental motivation ascribed to utilitarianism in Chapter III relates to the latter's particular view of what makes states of affairs (impersonally) good. If only the well-being or utility of individuals is relevant to such goodness, then the desire for good states of affairs can reduce to a kind of impersonal *benevolence*.

7 E.g., J. J. C. Smart in 'An outline of a system of utilitarian ethics', in *Utilitarianism: For and Against*, Cambridge University Press, 1973.

8 On this general topic, see Adams, *op. cit.*

9 The view being opposed here is explicitly defended in Parfit, *op. cit.* Incidentally, it is implausible to assume and, given our analysis of the example, it should not be assumed that saving the others would cause the loving parent to stop loving his child.

10 Compare Nagel, 'Subjective and Objective', esp. pp. 204f.

11 Cf. Adams, *op. cit.*, and A. K. Sen, 'Utilitarianism and Welfarism', *Journal of Philosophy*, 76, 1979, pp. 466f.

12 Presumably, these patterns should be thought of as allowing for and including intra-individual variation over time (with respect to motives, etc.) as well as differences (with respect to temporally variable motives, etc.) between individuals.

13 I assume that merely logical possibilities are no more relevant here than they are in act-utilitarianism and act-consequentialism generally. Note that our specification of the problem forces the assumption that less good would have been produced overall if the parent had never loved his child and had for that reason been willing to save the others. Cf. Adams, *op. cit.*, pp. 471ff.

14 Sen, *op. cit.*, p. 466n.

15 Our consideration of consequentialism thus raises issues concerning two different forms of impersonality, impersonality of the sort that considers things from the standpoint of no particular individual and impersonality that fails (or refuses) to evaluate agent-factors, i.e., person-factors, in separation from whatever else occurs, for better or worse, in the universe. The question raised here is whether the first form of impersonality, which is essential to the traditional consequentialist moral perspective, must invariably bring the second form of impersonality in its train and thereby undercut consequentialism as a distinctive form of moral theory. I assume that anything counting as a *moral* theory must not be impersonal in this second sense (way), but for some interesting caveats concerning this assumption, see Sen, *op. cit.*, pp. 465f.

CHAPTER VII COMMON-SENSE MORALITY AND THE FUTURE

1 '. . . this young man has lived for thirty years in the expectation of becoming a great writer, but this waiting itself is not enough: it becomes a vain and senseless obstinacy or a profound comprehension of his value according to the books which he writes.' (*Being and Nothingness*, New York, Philosophical Library, 1956, p. 539.) Sartre holds that this case illustrates the special nature of human freedom towards the future, but such an account lacks generality. It does not cover those cases (of which I shall give examples below) where the *past* makes a surprising difference to what we seem to be saying about the present. An explanation in terms of covert relationality allows us to handle Sartre's example and these other cases in a uniform manner.

2 Compare J. L. Mackie's notion of an '*inus* condition' (*The Cement of the Universe*, Oxford, Clarendon Press, 1974, p. 62). But of course Mackie is concerned with causal conditions, and we are here speaking of 'constitutive' conditions of states of affairs.

3 Here, as with our earlier discussion of 'has a profound comprehension . . .', mere potential is not sufficient to establish the applicability of the predicate in question. If a colony declares itself free and has the power to free itself from its rulers, but in the end decides to be reconciled with those rulers, the reconciliation will normally involve taking the declaration of independence as void *ab initio*. Saying 'but we had a republic there for a while' would be a sign that the rebels were *not* fully reconciled to the mother country.

4 And in other socio-political notions. Protestantism as a religious movement begins with Luther, rather than with Hus, for reasons having, again, to do with Luther's succeeding where Hus (in some sense) failed.

5 However, contrast Robert Nozick's opinion (in *Philosophical Explanations*, Cambridge, Mass., Harvard University Press, 1981, p. 45) that a watch that is disassembled at a watchmaker's (temporarily) ceases to exist. But disassembling a watch or building is different from scattering its parts to the winds. A judgment that the thing in question has been destroyed or no longer exists comes much easier in the latter case, and seems incompatible with saying that the thing exists *in storage* or *in a state of disassembly*.

6 See Nagel's 'Moral Luck', in *Mortal Questions*, Cambridge University Press, 1979, pp. 24–38. Even those objective utilitarians who make the rightness or wrongness of an action depend on actual results tend to treat notions like praise- and blameworthiness as applying in virtue of what it is reasonable for an agent to believe will happen rather than in virtue of what actually does happen.

7 I shall ignore the question of degrees of stupidity, but what I am saying could be reformulated to accommodate the intuitions of those who think the difference in stupidity between our two cases is a matter

of degree.

It is worth adding that, just as in some cases a republic exists no matter what comes later, some (extreme) forms of stupidity, negligence, and carelessness seem to count as such independently of anything that may occur subsequently. In the cases discussed in the text, by contrast, the inattentive driving falls within the limits of normal or average human driving – we all drive this way sometimes – so one is tempted to assign no moral fault at all if and when such driving has no bad consequences.

8 Or perhaps we should say instead that the mental and even, possibly, the inner are not as pure and unproblematic as categories as we are accustomed to thinking. Do the examples in the text tend to show that stupidity and the like involve something other than the inner (mental) and thus force us to rethink our opinions about what things truly *are* inner (mental); or should they persuade us, rather, that the inner (mental) can involve (what is normally thought of as) the outer (non-mental), with the result that (the usefulness, the coherence of) these categories themselves come into question? Compare Tyler Burge's 'Individualism and the Mental', in *Midwest Studies in Philosophy*, IV (*Studies in Metaphysics*), 1979, pp. 73–121. Burge also notes that Putnam's well-known views on the indexicality, etc., of terms like 'water' and 'elm' do *not* unambiguously persuade him (Putnam) either to rethink the idea of the mental (inner) or to hold that certain mental (inner) states involve factors outside a person's body.

9 In some cases whether we make a positive or a negative evaluation of what the sentry does will depend on (what we assume about) *earlier* events. If the woman has already done damage to his side, for example, letting her live (and escape punishment) will be seen as a wrongful, condemnable breach of duty once all the facts are known; but if she never does anything against his side, then it will be regarded as an instance of meritorious flexibility, etc. Even when an instance of moral luck fails to involve covert relationality *towards the future*, it may involve some other sort of covert relationality (cf. our later discussion of covert spatial relationality).

Incidentally, our differing moral judgments about the original sentry cases need not reflect differing assumptions about the woman's attitudes and intentions at the time the sentry spares her life. (If they did, our case for covert temporal relationality in the sentry examples would be undermined.) The woman may have no desire to harm his side when the sentry spares her life, but if she later, while housed in his army's camp, by sheer happenstance witnesses an incident which turns her against his side and persuades her to damage the camp, then it will be thought to have been wrong of him to let her live and enter the camp in the first place.

10 A diehard British chauvinist might even today think of the leaders of the revolution as traitors and of America itself as 'the Colonies'. But we would say of such a person that she was trying to turn the clock

back, and even such thinking reflects the connection between judgments of treason and judgments of existence.

11 See Goldman's 'Dated Rightness and Moral Imperfection', *Philosophical Review*, 85, 1977, pp. 449–87; and 'Doing the Best One Can', in A. Goldman and J. Kim, eds, *Values and Morals*, Dordrecht, Reidel, 1978, pp. 185–214, esp. p. 209; also see Sobel's 'Utilitarianism and Past and Future Mistakes', *Noûs*, X, 1976, pp. 195–219.

12 I leave aside all complications relating to the man's possible unwillingness to go through with the marriage if he subsequently learns of the woman's regret at having promised to marry him.

13 Our example is in fact more like cases where it is wrong to promise because one *can't* fulfil the promise, and where blame attaches to the promising rather than to the failure to fulfil, than like the above-mentioned cases where it is *wrong* to carry out a promise. On the other hand, where a promise cannot be carried out, it makes no sense to say, as in our own example, that the wrongfulness depends on whether it will actually be fulfilled.

14 Once we have the present example, it is not difficult to think of others where the significance, hence moral status, of some act of commitment, or even merely of communication, derives from subsequent actions on the part of its agent. For an interesting and (to my mind) convincing literary example of later actions determining the moral status of earlier ones, see Henry James's *The Ambassadors*. On the final page, James explicitly introduces the idea.

However, in *Philosophical Explanations* (p. 493) Nozick mentions a somewhat different case where the rightness or permissibility of an act may be thought to depend on its agent's subsequent behaviour. The case involves a person who is unjustly imprisoned and another person who steals a key from an innocent third party in order to effect his release. According to Nozick (as I understand him), the stealing is morally all right if the 'thief' subsequently makes an effort to release the prisoner, yet wrong if he simply throws away the key after stealing it. But it seems to me that one might just as plausibly – perhaps more plausibly – say that if the thief changes his mind after stealing the key and frivolously throws it away, it is this subsequent behaviour that is wrong or unjustified, not the original, morally-motivated act of stealing (of course, the thief may still have to make amends to the innocent party from whom he steals the key, but that is true even in the case where he releases the prisoner and where *ex hypothesi* it is not wrong on balance for him to steal the key). I think we do better to rely on the example in the main text above if we are looking for a case where a later act helps to determine the moral status of an earlier one. (Incidentally, someone might say of the key stealing case: he shouldn't have stolen the key if he was going to throw it away; but this hardly shows that we think the stealing was wrong in that case. After all, even when a promise was perfectly in order, we can always say, if it was not fulfilled: he shouldn't have made the promise if he wasn't going to fulfil it. Although the 'shouldn't' seems to govern (what is spoken of in) the first clause, it really governs the whole complex thought. What we have here is a somewhat misleading way of saying: making a certain promise and not keeping it is a wrong (conjunctive) act to perform. Compare: 'if he went to Bath, he couldn't have gone to Brighton'.)

15 Cf. note 9.

16 The qualification 'or immediate environment' reflects the possibility that we may (might) judge irreversibility and death in terms of readily available technology rather than in terms of what technology exists (somewhere) in the world at that time.

17 See, e.g., Ad Hoc Committee of the Harvard Medical School to Examine the Definition of Brain Death: a definition of irreversible coma, *Journal of the American Medical Association*, 205, 1968, pp. 337–40. For philosophical discussion, see John Ladd, 'The Definition of Death and the Right to Die', in J. Ladd, ed., *Ethical Issues Relating to Life and Death*, New York, Oxford University Press, 1979, pp. 126f.

18 See Burge, *op. cit.* For allusions to the idea of covert relationality, see Nozick, *op. cit.*, pp. 31–3. Nozick offers some examples of covert relationality towards the future but is hesitant (or unclear) about their status as such (see, e.g., pp. 44, 55).

19 Compare Davidson's view (in 'Mental Events', *Essays on Actions and Events*, Oxford University Press, 1980, esp. p. 221) that the attribution of mental states to agents is constitutively constrained by the need to make rational sense of an agent's total history of behaviour and that, in particular, 'the content of a propositional attitude derives from its place in the [agent's total] pattern [of actions and beliefs].' Here is a fairly clear commitment to the (covert) *temporal* relationality of *de dicto* belief predications.

INDEX

155

Index

International Library of Philosophy

Editor: Ted Honderich

(Demy 8vo)

Allen, R.E. (Ed.), **Studies in Plato's Metaphysics** *464 pp. 1965.* **Plato's 'Euthyphro' and the Earlier Theory of Forms** *184 pp. 1970.*

Allen, R.E. and Furley, David J. (Eds.), **Studies in Presocratic Philosophy**
   Vol. 1: The Beginnings of Philosophy *326 pp. 1970.*
   Vol. 11: Eleatics and Pluralists *448 pp. 1975.*

Armstrong, D.M., **Perception and the Physical World** *208 pp. 1961.* **A Materialist Theory of the Mind** *376 pp. 1967.*

Bambrough, Renford (Ed.), **New Essays on Plato and Aristotle** *184 pp. 1965.*

Barry, Brian, **Political Argument** *382 pp. 1965.*

Becker, Lawrence C. **On Justifying Moral Judgments** *212 pp. 1973.*

† Benenson, F.C., **Probability, Objectivity and Evidence** *224 pp. 1984.*

† * Blum, Lawrence, **Friendship, Altruism and Morality** *256 pp. 1980.*

Bogen, James, **Wittgenstein's Philosophy of Language** *256 pp. 1972.*

Brentano, Franz, **The Foundation and Construction of Ethics** *398 pp. 1973.*
   The Origin of our Knowledge of Right and Wrong *184 pp. 1969.*
   Psychology from an Empirical Standpoint *436 pp. 1973.*
   Sensory and Noetic Consciousness *168 pp. 1981.*

Broad, C.D., **Lectures on Psychical Research** *462 pp. 1962.*

† Clarke, D.S., **Practical Inferences** *160 pp. 1985.*

Crombie, I.M., **An Examination of Plato's Doctrine**
   Vol. 1: Plato on Man and Society *408 pp. 1962.*
   Vol. 11: Plato on Knowledge and Reality *584 pp. 1963.*

† Davies, Martin, **Meaning, Quantification, Necessity** *294 pp. 1981.*

Dennett, D.C., **Content and Conciousness** *202 pp. 1969.*

Detmold, M.J., **The Unity of Law and Morality** *288 pp. 1984.*

Dretske, Fred I., **Seeing and Knowing** *270 pp. 1969.*

Ducasse, C.J., **Truth, Knowledge and Causation** *264 pp. 1969.*

Fann. K.T. (Ed.), **Symposium on J.L. Austin** *512 pp. 1969.*

Findlay, J.N., **Plato: The Written and Unwritten Doctrines** *498 pp. 1974.*

† Findlay, J.N., **Wittgenstein: A Critique** *240 pp. 1984.*

Flew, Anthony, **Hume's Philosophy of Belief** *296 pp. 1961.*

† Fogelin, Robert J., **Skepticism and Naturalism in Hume's Treatise** *192 pp. 1985.*

† Foster, John, **The Case for Idealism** *280 pp. 1982.*

Glover, Jonathan, **Responsibility** *212 pp. 1970.*

Goldman, Lucien, **The Hidden God** *424 pp. 1964.*

† Gray, John, **Mill on Liberty: A Defence** *160 pp. 1983.*

Hamlyn, D.W., **Sensation and Perception** *222 pp. 1961.*

† Honderich, Ted (Ed.), **Morality and Objectivity** *256 pp. 1985.*

† * Hornsby, Jennifer, **Actions** *152 pp. 1980.*

Husserl, Edmund, **Logical Investigations** *Vol. 1: 456 pp.*
   Vol. 11: 464 pp. 1970.